Always

a
Princess

OTHER BOOKS AND AUDIO BOOKS

BY MEG JOHNSON

When Life Gets Hard . . . (Live talk on CD and book)

Let Your Light Shine (Live talk on CD)

Life isn't always a
fairy tale, but you are . . .

Always

a
Princess

Meg Johnson

Covenant Communications, Inc.

Cover image: *Glass Slipper* © DNY59, istockphotography.com

Cover design copyright © 2013 by Covenant Communications, Inc.

Published by Covenant Communications, Inc.
American Fork, Utah

Printed in the United States of America
First Printing: August 2013

19 18 17 16 15 14 13   10 9 8 7 6 5 4 3 2 1

ISBN 978-1-62108-342-9

For princesses everywhere . . .

Chapter 1
INTRODUCTION

DOPEY FORGOT.

That was the excuse I used to explain why that particular dwarf wasn't with me. I was fifteen years old, playing Snow White at a seven-year-old's birthday party, and didn't have a single dwarf to back me up. But I had excuses for all of the dwarves' absences: Doc had an appointment. Sleepy slept in. I was pretty sure Bashful was right behind me, but . . . .

The seven-year-old birthday girl was the daughter of a local theater director. I was playing Snow White in a play he was directing called *Into the Woods*. I was much younger than any of the other actors but looked enough like the fair-skinned princess that the director cast me.

I diligently attended weekly rehearsals, where we sang and danced and practiced scene blocking. I spent hours at these play practices and then waited for what seemed like more hours for my mom to come pick me up when it was over. I guess that was the breaks when I was fifteen—no license and lots of waiting.

We performed at an amphitheater, and I went early (er, had my mom drop me off early . . . .) each night of the two-week-long performance run so I could perfect my make-up and costume.

All this for a whopping three minutes of stage time.

It was tough to be a princess.

My performance consisted of coming out with my dashing prince, yawning, and then singing the finale with the rest of the cast. My youth and inexperience showed dramatically in my singing, and the music director kept changing me from soprano to alto and then back to soprano as she tried to match my "skills."

Surely, every "real" princess knew how to sing perfectly, right? Well, I suppose I looked real enough for my three minutes in the finale.

And I must have looked real enough to convince seven-year-olds because a week after closing night, the director called and offered me fifty dollars to play Snow White at his daughter's birthday party. Snow White can *always* use an extra fifty.

Besides getting slightly richer, being a princess—a real, live princess, according to the awestruck little girls—made me feel a little, well, cool. I mean, after all, I had the right hair, the right make-up, the right dress, and the right yawn for the occasion. I was right on, and everyone there (all of the excited little seven-year-old party guests) knew it.

It felt good to be the princess of the party. Really good.

But seven-year-old birthday parties are the exception. In real life, it seems like we are the princess of the party only if we are right on with the right hair, right make-up, and right dress for the right occasion. If we're off even a little bit, it's over. Done. We lose.

Just imagine Snow White, regal in her yellow and blue dress with the high white collar framing her round, pale face and brown hair.

Oops.

While the seven-year-olds might have noticed my hair, they still accepted me as the actual Snow White, while anyone older might have called me out on the fact that my hair wasn't black—just dark brown. Anyone older might also have known that the real Snow White had brown eyes; mine were green. Anyone older would have been just a little better at determining *who* the princess *really* was . . . and wasn't.

The real princess is the girl who is right on. Right on with the right hair, right on with the right make-up, right on with the right designer jeans and right on with the fancy jewelry.

And sometimes—just sometimes—the scepter falls to us. And we love it!

There are so few times that we feel like we're socially right on, so when it happens, we get excited. Something as simple as a Paparazzi party, where we happen to be seated closest to the hostess and we happen to know the latest gossip, gets us all riled up in that royal feeling.

Then afterward, once we return to our castle in suburbia, the princess status and the royal feeling wear off. They never last. In our less-than-royal rags, we accept our peasant position and forego the visions of happily ever after.

With time, the perfect, pretty-princess feeling completely disappears. That's when we start to reminisce about the royal feelings from yesteryear when we knew there were times we were right on with our perfect hair, perfect make-up, and perfect clothes that fit perfectly over our perfect bodies. It's gone for us now though. That royal feeling rode off into the sunset—without us.

We'd like to forget it and move on with our broader hips—I mean, perspectives—but we keep reviving it with every little girl we see. We constantly encourage younger generations to dress up as, act like, and believe they are princesses.

Perhaps we should just let Sleeping Beauty lie, but we forge ahead to set her and all of her perfect princess friends free with every pink bow and tiara and "Isn't she a little princess?" comment. No longer princesses ourselves, we fight the dragons that would dampen the royal mood of any seven-year-old's plastic tea party—even if we don't have kids. We can't bear to tell them the words *Official Princess* printed on a T-shirt are probably not legit because we feel obligated to preserve that royal feeling we once felt in every new generation of tutu-donning tykes. We preserve it for those who can hold a conversation with a plush turtle. We preserve it for those without deadlines. Without dependents. Without pragmatism. That royal feeling is for those who can get away with wearing light-up sneakers and pigtails under dollar-store crowns.

That royal feeling isn't for us because we know too much now about what makes and breaks someone's "right on" princess status. However, we continue to feed little girls' imaginations (and their stuffed animal party guests') with diamond-crusted princess fodder until they can't swallow another morsel. They usually reach their max when they too grow out of their princess pajamas . . . and grow into us.

We know. We know because that royal feeling is gone for anyone who cares that the tea in the plastic teapot came from the garden hose. That royal feeling is gone for anyone who has to comb through someone else's royal mess of tangles. And that royal feeling is gone for anyone who considers checking themselves into a mental hospital after carrying on a lively conversation with a stuffed animal.

The princess-only train ride is short. Next stop: maturity. Thanks for traveling. Please step off quickly. Leave your royal feeling on board.

In short, the royal feeling is not for any of us who are old enough to know that tutus are for ballerinas and light-up sneakers don't come in our size.

The royal feeling isn't for me.

The royal feeling isn't for you.

Right?

I mean, how can *anyone* feel royal when completely unroyal things happen to them? Like flat tires and overdrafts and shopping lists. How can anyone feel like a princess when she feels more like the wicked witch because she had to momentarily crash the tea party because the chocolate crumpet frosting smelled weird and she didn't remember frosting any crumpets . . . .

And *still*, we, in our ten-year-old sneakers (that don't light up) and a T-shirt worn for the second day in a row (because it is the only one that fits just right, right now), return the princess train to its tracks and send it choo-chooing on its way—despite the fact that we're not allowed on it.

We can't board the train because, while the princess train riders sing lalala to every magic woodland creature, the only animal attracted to us is the muddy neighborhood dog who really loves the front flower bed— but not the entire bed, just the part where your most recently planted flowers are. He's a very smart dog.

We can't board the princess-only train because when princess train riders think "castle," we think "rambler." When they think "chariot," we think "minivan." And when they think "tidy up," we think "Saturday chores overhaul worked to the tune of '*Why doesn't anyone know where the sink is except me?*'"

And while the tiny-tot princess train rides blissfully to the unknown land of Happily-Ever-After, we wonder when it will derail—hopefully not before she outgrows her extremely expensive princess sneakers with the pink laces . . . .

And though many don't really care that light-up sneakers don't come in size seven and a half, we continue to stare longingly into the sunset, wondering what in the world happened to our own happily ever after. We stepped off the princess train long ago, leaving our plastic crowns behind. We just can't muster that royal feeling anymore.

It's difficult to feel it because we have to handle non-princess-like things. Like muffin tops, bad breath, day-old hair, and dark circles. I never see princesses with any of these—ever. Not in a book, not in a movie, not even at any theme park. Don't princesses have dark circles? I never see any of them even applying make-up . . . .

And cereal dregs. I really can't imagine any fairytale princess waking up in her evening-gown pajamas and gliding gracefully into her quaint kitchen to pour herself a crystal bowl full of the last bit of cereal dust topped off with a dainty helping of almost-expired milk.

Oh, no, not fairytale princesses. They have an endless supply of never-crumbled cereal and expirationless milk. And no dark circles. They blissfully wander through their enchanted forests with their magical friends, awaiting their assured happily ever after.

"Happily ever after" is supposedly a future occurrence, but the more into the future I go, the farther I feel from it. It seemed as if my happily ever after was closer at fifteen when I was Snow White making up excuses for the absence of my dwarves than it is now.

Life has definitely taken some unexpected turns and left me feeling much differently than my princess mind thought I would at this point. I definitely was no pretty princess when I woke up at age twenty-two, broken and dirty, facedown in the red sand of Southern Utah.

I had been hiking, jumping from boulder to boulder, and accidentally jumped off the cliff face. I broke both of my legs and both of my arms. I broke my collar bone, and I broke my neck.

In the hospital, they pronounced me a quadriplegic, paralyzed from the chest down without the use of my hands. The doctors told me I would be in a wheelchair for the rest of my life.

Princesses are *not* in wheelchairs.

But girls are. I mean, sometimes. Not *all* girls, but regular girls like me can be in wheelchairs and totally rock them! Don't get me wrong; it took quite a bit of the ugly cry (and I am sure you're familiar with the ugly cry) to overcome the fact that my princess train had been obliterated and I'd never be right on in any social situation again. But once I came to terms with the other side of awful—and the other side of walking—I knew everything was okay.

As I began to reenter my life in a wheelchair, I joined the Utah wheelchair rugby team: the Scorpions. The practices and games were intense, and even though I enjoyed wheelchair rugby, I realized sports just weren't my thing. Everyone's got some kind of thing, but since I was newly paralyzed, I didn't know what mine was, other than I was pretty sure it wasn't rugby.

As I looked around, though, I discovered that sports were nearly the only available activity for people in wheelchairs—tennis, golf, basketball, rugby—and it wasn't as if I was going to magically love sports just because they were the only activities available.

I looked for other opportunities available for girls in wheelchairs, and I came across the Ms. Wheelchair America Pageant. Even though I had never done pageants before, I knew I *had* to be a part of it.

I wanted to wear beautiful dresses and have beautiful hair. I wanted to be feminine and dainty. I wanted to feel beautiful.

I immediately called the national Ms. Wheelchair America Board and asked how I could participate.

When I got someone on the other end, I said, "I'm Meg! I'm from Utah! What do I have to do to be able to come?"

I heard a cold, distant voice reply, "Oh. You're from *Utah*. Well, Utah doesn't have a state pageant. And you have to be a state winner to come to Ms. Wheelchair America. I'm sorry. You can't come."

What? My heart sank a little.

Fine.

So I got off the phone.

And then I got on eBay . . . and I bought myself a crown!

And I called back the Ms. Wheelchair America Board and introduced myself. "Hello. *I* am Ms. Wheelchair Utah."

So they let me come.

I participated in the 2006 Ms. Wheelchair America Pageant in New York, where I represented Utah as an independent delegate.

When I competed at the pageant, I had only been paralyzed for sixteen months—I remember because my speech started out, *I've been paralyzed for sixteen months and sixteen days . . . .* There were thirty-five contestants there, and I was the newest to a wheelchair and one of the youngest.

On one of the first nights of the pageant, they ended dinner and cleared the floor for "dancing." As many of the contestants rolled around the floor in their wheelchairs to the music, doing, I suppose, their weird version of what I'd always known "dancing" to be, I felt tears well up in my eyes. I loved to dance. But dancing, I thought, was only something legs could do. I thought these wheelchair girls looked silly. They were barely moving. But as the music played louder and the contestants looked like they were having more and more fun, I decided there was only so much time I was allowed to sit on the sidelines of my life. So I joined them, and I danced until my arms were tired.

I had a great time at the Ms. Wheelchair America Pageant. It lasted a week and was full of seminars and classes, dinners, dancing, shows, and, oh yeah, pageant stuff. During one my interviews with the five judges, I was a little intimidated because I felt as if they were elevated (maybe I was just feeling small). They peered over the judges' table and seemed to look down at me as they asked their questions—not easy ones like, "What's your favorite color," or "How do you like your eggs," but hard ones like, "So how do you feel about the ADA laws in Utah?"

Um . . . the what?

My intellectually lacking response didn't quite impress them, but my initiative to be there and passion for life did. They presented the Spirit Award to me during the closing ceremony.

After I returned home, my boyfriend (who is now my husband) and I founded the Ms. Wheelchair Utah Pageant, and we now send winners annually to compete in the Ms. Wheelchair America Pageant. It feels good to provide girls in wheelchairs opportunities to wear beautiful dresses and have beautiful hair and just feel beautiful.

I still have the crown I bought myself. It is not the crown we pass from titleholder to titleholder—*that* particular crown is huge and heavy and shiny and gorgeous, a gift from a family friend. No, my little crown is small and fragile and not very elaborate. It's simple. If I were to compare it to myself, there would be a lot of similarities. It's small, and I feel small. It's fragile, and I feel fragile. It's currently broken and missing some rhinestones, but it still shines. Again, that's much the way I feel.

Sometimes I put it on when I'm by myself. I mean, it just feels cool to have a crown on my head and feel like a princess (don't pretend like you haven't done that). I've been tempted to wear it out, not to anyplace embarrassing, just out to a fancy restaurant or something, but I'm pretty sure I'd get weird looks.

But I definitely wouldn't get as many weird looks as *you* would get. See, a girl in a wheelchair can get away with slightly crazy stuff like that. If people question, they just assume we have brain damage or a terminal disease and we're simply out on the town, checking items off our bucket list. Most everything we people in wheelchairs do seems to be okay and acceptable. But on the other hand, if you were to wear a crown to your favorite restaurant, you would probably get the "that is a total social faux pas" look from everyone who sees you. You'd be scrutinized and visually dismissed by princess-status assessors everywhere. You would definitely not be right on.

But would you be wrong?

I'm pretty sure you don't have a moat in your front lawn. I'm pretty sure you don't have a pea hidden under your mattress (well, not on purpose anyway). And I'm pretty sure you'd run like crazy if a bird flew into your hair and attempted to style it.

I'm pretty sure that as far as storybook princesses go, you're not "right on."

But the question remains: if you wore a crown, would you be wrong?

That is the real question. We begin singing "I Am a Child of God" in our Primary years. Young Women are taught that they are "daughters of our Heavenly Father, who loves [them]." The Relief Society motto begins, "We are beloved spirit daughters of God." No matter our age, we are reminded of who we are: children of God. We are daughters of our Heavenly Father, the *King*.

And what do you call the daughter of the King?

President Dieter F. Uchtdorf of the First Presidency said, "You are truly royal spirit daughters of Almighty God. You are princesses, destined to become queens."[1] It all comes together royally in one fell swoop. Being a princess isn't a fairy tale. It isn't a fantasy. It isn't a future occurrence or something we grow out of. We are and will always be daughters of the King. We are princesses.

This isn't me trying to make you feel good by including a cute quote I think you'll like and can post on your bathroom mirror. This isn't a peppy motivational speaker trying to boost your self-esteem. This isn't your mom buoying up her little princess, trying to keep her on the princess-only train just a bit longer. This is an apostle of the Lord speaking truth, telling us we that are daughters of God, daughters of the Eternal King.

Someday we will write the final pages of our stories on earth, and our mortal lives will come to a close. If we have proven worthy, we will live forever in our happily ever after with God, and we will be like Him.

But right now, we're between the dusty covers of our princess storybooks, separated by the veil from the memories of our royal home. And here, between the dog-eared, weathered pages, it's hard to remember we are princesses when our heavenly palace and King feel so far away.

I attended a large Youth Spectacular Celebration at Weber State University in Ogden, Utah. Young men and women from thirty stakes sang, danced, and bore testimony on the football field as thousands

---

1   Uchtdorf, Dieter F., "Your Happily Ever After," *Ensign*, May 2010, 127.

watched from the stands. During the opening scene, hundreds of youth in white robes stood on one side of the field and represented all of us in the premortal existence. A tarp painted like the world lay on the other side of the field, and several more youth stood along the fifty-yard line waving blue flowing fabric as a representation of the veil. Then the hundreds of white-robed youth ran at what seemed like full speed through the flowing blue veil, shedding their white robes to reveal T-shirts and shorts as they excitedly came to earth.

As I watched them, a long-forgotten memory pricked my mind of when I left the premortal existence and came through the veil to this world.

Literally.

In a flashing moment, my mind's eye saw me sitting one-on-one with Heavenly Father. I knew I was just about to come to earth. He had His arms around me, and I heard myself make one last request: "Please, don't let me forget."

Though I know He will not, on this side of the veil, it is hard to remember just where we came from and harder still to remember who we are. We have a sense that we're royal, but we have a hard time applying our intuition. Our clothes get fancier and fancier as we search to satisfy our princess craving. Each magazine cover shows off the prettiest princess who flaunts her happily-ever-after façade. We go to the most happening social events we can, though often the extent of our social calendar is the grocery store and our efforts to look royally presentable seem insufficient for the deciding eyes of society. And in our shopping around for where we fit in, we return home with only a carton of 2% confidence.

And so we, in our not-so-pretty-princess life, with our suburbia castle and favorite frumpy outfit, need to remember who we are.

We are daughters of Heavenly Father. Who loves us. And we love Him.

And we miss Him.

So while we can't reach up to give Him a hug, we *can* blow Him a kiss.

To do this, we just have to remember K.I.S.S: be Kind, see Individual Worth, Sing, and Smile. These simple acts open the door between our King and us so He can extend His hand to remind us of our princess status. They are how we build His kingdom here to create a small resemblance of our heavenly home.

As we build God's kingdom, it won't matter how long it's been since we were passengers on the princess-only train, and it won't matter how not right our hair is or how not right our clothes are; blowing a kiss to Heavenly Father and doing His work offers a royal feeling and reminds us of our royal heritage.

Each time we open the door and blow a kiss, Heavenly Father will remind us that He is the King and we are His daughters—His princesses— here on earth.

Chapter 2
KINDNESS

As we are kind to others, Heavenly Father will show kindness to us.

Old-Fashioned Kindness

KINDNESS IS THE FIRST STEP as we blow a kiss to our Heavenly Father. Kindness seems (and is) so simple, but for whatever reason, kindness seems to be out of date and just a little old fashioned. It has become a social faux pas, and in social circles, one who is kind is considered weak.

In the race of life, it seems that if we have time to slow down to help another runner, surely our to-do list is too short, our social contributions too small, and our friends too few in number. It appears that if we take time to show kindness, we don't have enough to do.

However, behaving stressed and frazzled seems to put on a show that we have *much* to do and are *very* important. A woman who appears drained and hurried must be a prominent person. As tension rises in a woman so does her social significance.

Right?

When I was a teenager, I thought a lack of kindness manifested itself only among young women. I looked forward to growing up and having everyone "just get along." My junior high and high school years were speckled with unkind peers. Backbiting, teasing, and passive-aggressive bullying were prevalent.

In junior high, a couple of the girls in my ward didn't seem to like me. Activities, conferences, firesides, and especially camps were great opportunities for them to show their dislike. Once after a mutual activity, I came back to the church classroom to get my backpack and found its contents strewn between several classrooms. I gathered my stuff and walked home. Alone.

I began to see a correlation between a lack of kindness and popularity. A little later in my teenage years, I took my newfound knowledge to heart. I learned how to be just unkind enough to keep myself ahead socially. I had to be "just unkind enough" because *too kind* would make me weak and *too unkind* would make me rude. So *balance* was the key to proper unkindness.

I had to be subtle.

I mean, I couldn't be outright rude; that was too transparent, especially when I got a little older. I had to do it sneakily. Passive-aggressively.

That was the *classy* way to do it.

By the time I was in my late teens, I had grown into a seasoned social leader who was just harsh enough and just unkind enough to be popular. I remember one instance when I was rehearsing with my dance company and saw another dance teacher and a few of her dancers enter through the glass doors. I zeroed in on one of the dancers. I had seen her several times before, and she was really pretty *and* a good dancer. We were about the same size and had similar technique skills. And I didn't like her. At all.

My dance choreographer sometimes invited other teams to learn and perform dances with us, and I liked this visiting team the least because of this one girl. When another dancer was as good as me and looked like me, she became competition because the choreographer had to choose between the two of us for the spot in the dance where he needed our height and skill.

This visiting dancer was going down, and I took every opportunity to remind her that she was in *my* dance hall and it was *my* turf and she was *my* guest!

But I had to take all of these "opportunities" at the right moment, in subtle, crafty ways. I was the queen of that dance hall, and no queen was outright rude. I had to put her down passive-aggressively, in the *classy* way.

During a water break, I was coming back into the hall when I saw her sitting alone on a bench. I took this one-on-one chance to let her know— again—how unimportant and small she was, especially to me. I decided to pretend like I'd forgotten her name. We had been introduced several times and had danced together often. We had even been cast in the same Broadway musical review. I *knew* her name. But I thought pretending like I'd forgotten her name would be a good way to reiterate her unimportance. I thought this classy unkindness would squish her under my split-sole jazz sneakers.

Smiling, I approached her. With overly nice, sugar-dripping words, I said hello and told her I was glad she could come to *my* dance hall. I then asked her name—again (oh, I just had *too many* visiting dancers to keep track of).

It's been many years since that day, but I remember almost every detail perfectly, as if it just happened. I can see the dimly lit room and the cream-colored, high-back bench where she sat. I remember wiping away water from my face because the water fountain squirted high. I remember how I was standing when I asked her what her name was. I remember all of this, but as ironic as it is, I can't remember her name.

Though I'll never forget what she said.

After she kindly told me her name, she smiled and, with bright, sparkling eyes, added, "And you're Meg. I could never forget you. You're unforgettable."

Gulp.

I don't remember how I responded. I just remember looking for a rock to climb under so I could hide. I walked back into the dance hall with my head hung low. Her words stung. Not because she was being sarcastic but because she wasn't.

Writer Joseph Joubert said, "A part of kindness consists in loving people more than they deserve."[2] My actions were not lovable, but that dancer showed me love anyway. This girl was truly kind. I will never forget that moment, looking into her happy face as she smiled sincerely and showed me the love I didn't deserve.

I had gone out of my way to put her down, and in return, she had gone out of her way to lift me up. She had gone out of her way to make me feel good when it was clear to both of us, I'm sure, that I had intended to be mean to show her the real princess of that dance hall.

In the end, I *did* show her the real princess: her. Because she showed kindness when it was undeserved, she emphasized a trait of true royalty. A *true* princess rises above the hurtful, hateful, and spiteful unkindness of others. She is humble when haughty is easier. She is smiley when scowly is more natural. She is pleasant when prideful is the first reaction.

The writer Elbert Hubbard described true princess kindness the best when he said, "Strong men can always afford to be gentle. Only the weak are intent on 'giving as good as they get.'"[3] I was weak in my front of put-downs and harsh, unnecessary intimidation, but this unnamed dancer was the strong one. She was the kind one. She was the princess.

Sister Margaret D. Nadauld, former General Young Women president, shared the characteristics of a true princess: "Women of God can never be

---

2   In Flaherty, Patrick, *The Scout Law—Quotes for Life* (Bettendorf, IA: Teckni-Corp), 49.

3   Hubbard, Elbert, *The Notebook of Elbert Hubbard* (USA: Roycrofters, 1927), 135.

like women of the world. The world has enough women who are tough; we need women who are tender. There are enough women who are coarse; we need women who are kind. There are enough women who are rude; we need women who are refined. We have enough women of fame and fortune; we need more women of faith. We have enough greed; we need more goodness. We have enough vanity; we need more virtue. We have enough popularity; we need more purity."[4]

Each of us has a dual personality: our inner princess and the natural man. They battle daily. The inner princess wants to share with and love and hug strangers at the zoo, while the natural man wants to throw that pushy guy who side-stepped in front of our kid into the bear pit. It is a neverending struggle, and there is only one winner at a time.

Which one will win today?

There is no room in our princess lives for the natural man. The more difficult it is to show kindness to someone, the more important it is that we do so. The harder it is to act like a princess, the more like a princess you'll feel when you actually do it—and slowly, your princess self will overpower the natural man!

One of my biggest trials in overcoming the natural man is behaving like a princess when I'm driving. I often use a particular freeway on-ramp. It is a left-hand turn with two lanes that quickly merge into one, and I am relatively certain that in addition to being a freeway on-ramp, it is also a try-out track for the next Indy-500 race.

At this on-ramp, everyone guns their engines and goes as fast as possible to beat the car next to them onto the on-ramp. Their reward is that they get to be before that particular car as we all merge into one lane and drive onto the freeway—and they may or may not receive a phone call from our friends at Indy.

I'm not going to lie—I love to race at that particular light. I *love* when I'm the first car in one of the lanes. I *love* to slam on the gas (with my hand controls) when the light turns green. And I *love* to be the first car down the ramp. It's a rush and a total cheap thrill. I'm expecting a call from Indy any day now . . . .

But when I'm not the first car in the starting line and I'm stuck behind another car, maybe more than one, and I have to merge in with everyone else like a zipper, and if the car in front of me goes slowly, I watch helplessly as the other line of cars flies by and they get two or three cars in

---

4 Nadauld, Margaret D., "The Joy of Womanhood," *Ensign*, Nov. 2000.

before another one from our line gets a chance to merge. Unless I'm first, I can't go faster than the next car, and I get frustrated with the slower cars.

This is where bad words are born.

And even when both lines of cars (I call them teams) are moving smoothly together and zippering in systematically (their team, our team, their team . . . .), sometimes someone from either team will be greedy and not wait for their turn to zipper in appropriately, so they tailgate their team member to eliminate room for the other team's car—usually *mine*—to zipper in.

This is where inappropriate gestures are born. (Having paralyzed hands doesn't take the temptation away.)

All of this just to get on the freeway.

Recently, as I was getting on the freeway at this on-ramp, I was in line behind some cars, trying to zipper into one lane with the other team. As we started to go, we were all playing fairly and taking turns, but then someone on the other team was selfish and tailgated the car in front so I couldn't zipper in appropriately.

I started to get really mad at them, and the natural man inside me fumed. *How rude!* I thought. *How egotistical! How self-centered!* I wondered how someone could feel so high and mighty and not care at all that someone else might have somewhere to be. *She didn't even think to consider that I might be running late or that I maybe have had a bad day!* As I stared the other driver down with a glaring scowl, a thought occurred to me that I had never before considered: I was the selfish one.

What? I thought. *No way.* She *is!*

But all of those characteristics I had used to describe the other driver described *me*. I was the rude one for insisting I should be first. I was egotistical for believing my errand was more important than hers. I was self-centered in thinking *my* plans, *my* agenda, and *my* life were more important.

I was the one who was cut off . . . and *I* was the one who was unkind.

Since that realization, I look at "rude" drivers with new eyes—the beautiful Bambi kind of eyes with unbelievably long eyelashes. When I am cut off or flipped off or honked at or frowned at, I smile back and bat my lashes and let my heart swell with love for them and sympathy for their hard day—I know they've had one—because it's probably been a lot like mine. Long. Tiring. And they just want to go home. We *all* just want to go home.

Home—our celestial home—can feel just a little closer as we allow our hearts to swell with kindness and love for others, even (and especially) when kindness is undeserved and difficult to offer. As we show kindness to others, Heavenly Father will show kindness to us. He will remind us whose daughters we are. He will treat us like princesses.

Princess Power

Superman can see through walls. Spider-Man can shoot webs. And we princesses show kindness. We have that secret superpower, and it's all our own! It might not seem very intimidating, and no one would ever write an entire comic book series about it, but kindness *is* the princess superpower. And its powers rival any comic book hero's.

We sisters in Zion and the sisters of the rest of the world have this princess superpower in common, but our skill to use it varies. Like anything else in life, we can improve our kindness proficiency as we practice using it, especially on our foes.

We all have a foe, a nemesis, if you will. We all have someone in our lives who excels at chastising our peace. No matter how nice our family, how loving our neighbors, or how wonderful our ward, we have all known—and will know—someone who isn't quite as nice, as loving, or as wonderful.

It may seem the actions (or lack thereof) of these not-nice, unloving, and unwonderful people don't deserve kindness—from anyone. Maybe this person is offensive, rude, or mean. Maybe this person is hypocritical, too analytical, or a pathological liar.

They can start young, but they have no age limit. When I was starting junior high school, I moved to Utah and became friends with Erin, a girl my age who lived down the street. We carpooled to school every day. A couple months into our seventh-grade year, Erin told me how one of her friends at school, Cassidy, hated my guts.

I was really confused. I didn't even know who Cassidy was. The next school day, I had Erin point her out to me. I was still confused. I didn't have any classes with Cassidy, and I didn't remember talking to, sitting by, or even passing by her at all. I wondered what I could have done that had made her dislike me so much.

I know I am not alone when I say that it really bothers me when someone dislikes me. I know I can't please *everyone*, but I don't want to give anyone a legitimate reason to not like me. And it really made me feel bad that Cassidy, someone I didn't know at all, disliked me to the point of hating my guts.

I wanted to fix whatever bad impression I'd given Cassidy, but I felt more strongly that I just didn't want her to have it in the first place. I mean, really, what was her problem? I was brand new to the school—to the state—and she hated my guts before we'd even had a conversation? In that moment, I really wanted to give her a good reason to hate my guts . . . .

It's hard to use our princess superpower. When we've been wronged, it's a lot easier to respond in an eye-for-an-eye and tooth-for-a-tooth and if-you-hate-my-guts-then-I-hate-yours manner, but that's weak. It isn't the princess way. Princesses can't be weak, even though we reeeeeally want to be on occasion. We must be strong—and strength tastes bad sometimes. For extra strength, Popeye had to swallow canned spinach, and for our princess superpower to be effective, we have to swallow our pride. Sometimes I think I'd rather eat cold canned spinach.

But with Cassidy, I swallowed my pride, and I began going out of my way to find her in the hallway between classes and at lunch time. When I saw her, I smiled big and said hi.

I planned to do it until the day I died, but as it turned out, I only had to do it for a few days before my friend Erin told me the good news—Cassidy liked me! Cassidy said she had been wrong about me and I was, in fact, very kind. We became friends.

Awww, what a happy ending.

Since my time in junior high, I have learned that there is a name for what I did. It is "killing with kindness," which is the most effective way to calm the storms that rage in relationships (or the little drizzles that pour down on friends before they become friends). Kindness can kill the nastiest feelings between siblings just as easily as it can kill tension between colleagues and spouses.

In discussing the effects of exercising our princess superpower, Joseph B. Wirthlin said, "Kindness is the essence of greatness and the fundamental characteristic of the noblest men and women I have known. Kindness is a passport that opens doors and fashions friends. It softens hearts and molds relationships that can last lifetimes . . . . Kindness is the essence of a celestial life. Kindness is how a Christlike person treats others. Kindness should permeate all of our words and actions at work, at school, at church, and especially in our homes."[5]

As we run alongside others in our daily race, let's unabashedly use our princess superpower on all of them, whether we need to kill a yucky feeling or create a pleasant one. The power behind a quickly forgotten kind word can be unforgettable for the person who hears it.

---

5 Wirthlin, Joseph B., "The Virtue of Kindness," *Ensign*, May 2005.

Our Duty to be Kind

In my second summer of being in a wheelchair, I signed up to race in a 5k on the Fourth of July.

My arms were not very strong, and I was not very fast, but I practiced diligently for the race. I rolled around my neighborhood every day, building strength and growing in confidence—even if ever so slightly.

On the day of the race, I was so excited I couldn't stand it. (It's a good thing I was sitting.) I checked in, got my free race T-shirt, and immediately put it on. I went outside, where hundreds of racers were stretching and warming up. I didn't want to look out of place, so I started stretching my arms and looking pumped.

There were lots of girls, all in cute running clothes and sleek running shoes. I looked down at my lifeless legs, clad in cargo shorts and sandals. Even though I didn't need my legs or feet to run the race, I started thinking that I should have at least dressed right. I shifted uncomfortably in my free racing T-shirt when I discovered that, apparently, it wasn't very cool to put it on first thing.

The other racers had cute hair pulled back in tight ponytails. Mine was styled in my regular short, flippy bob, and I had on full make-up. Being a quadriplegic, I don't sweat, so my make-up and hair would be as good after the race as before.

The runners seemed to be clustered in groups, chatting and smiling together as they warmed up. But no one was sitting with me. No one was stretching with me. No one was chatting with me. Alone, I stretched my arms some more, trying to look like I belonged. As runners passed me in short warm-up jogs, I smiled at them, hoping to get some encouragement back, but no one looked. My heart fluttered with embarrassment, and I tried to remind myself that they were nervous too. I mean, it *was* a race after all.

An announcer shouted that the race was about to begin. The hoard of runners crowded the starting line. I tried to push to the line too, but I kept getting cut off by other runners who were eager to be closer. Seamlessly, runner after runner stepped in front of me, and soon, I was at the very back, just barely in front of three plump ladies pushing their kids in strollers—obviously just there for the exercise.

I was getting frustrated. Didn't the other runners see me? What was their problem? No one was taking me seriously, and I was starting to think that maybe I wasn't taking myself seriously either.

What was I even doing here?

As I looked at the swarm of people in front of me, I choked down a lump in my throat. What was I thinking signing up for this race? I wasn't wearing the right shoes, the right shorts, or the right shirt. I didn't even have a racing wheelchair. I was just in my regular ol' one.

My efforts to squeeze back tears were futile, and they escaped from my eyes. Luckily, no one noticed my seventh circle of self-consciousness, and the gunshot exploded through the air.

As the race began, I shook my head, hoping the embarrassment would dissipate, and I pushed hard on my wheels. I went faster and faster, but faster and faster for me wasn't fast enough, and my effort was only enough to keep up with the moms with strollers—who were chatting and laughing together, clearly not taking this event seriously.

And even *they* were passing me.

What was I even doing? I thought. What was I even thinking? I couldn't even keep ahead of the people who weren't even trying!

But *I* was trying. And all of my trying was for nothing. All of my effort—everything I had—kept me in very last place. I was losing. And I felt like a loser.

A bicyclist team rode past me. They had stopped their bike ride to let the crowd of runners make their way off the starting line. I sighed and supposed that they thought everyone in the race was well on their way already.

I lowered my head and hid my face, not wanting any of them to laugh at "the wheelchair girl in the runner's shirt" who was ten feet behind the moms who were walking with their strollers. I didn't want them to see my pink cheeks. I didn't want them to see me crying. I didn't want them to see me at all. But the last bicyclist slowed down so as not to pass me. She came uncomfortably close, and I thought she hadn't seen me. She steered her bicycle so it was coming closer to me, and I had to veer away from her and toward the curb so she wouldn't hit me.

I was struggling to get out of her way. *C'mon, lady!* I said in my head. *Leave me alone. Can't you see me?*

But she got right up next to me, leaned over, and, just loud enough for me to hear, whispered, "You're cool."

My heart beamed. I stopped pushing and looked up as she rode away.

With renewed vigor, I put my hands on my wheels. I leaned forward and squinted at the stroller moms ahead. I let out a miniature roar (you can do things like that when everyone has passed you). I pushed forward, and I pushed hard.

I refused to quit. I pushed for the bicyclist. I needed to be as cool as she thought I was. She thought I was cool, and I was starting to believe her.

Mark Twain said, "I can live for two months on a good compliment."[6] The same goes for me. Those two short words from that kind woman resounded in my head for five kilometers—and beyond.

I could hear her again and again with every push as I strained to catch up to the stroller moms. *You're cool. You're cool. You're cool.* With every effort and every struggle, which were many along the route, I heard her words over and over: *You're cool.*

Almost forty-five minutes later, I finished that race just behind the stroller moms.

Dead last.

But they gave me first place in the wheelchair division.

In our daily race, we often feel like we're behind every other racer and in last place. We feel lonely, self-conscious, and foolish. We need something—anything—to help us along, and we often find a kind visiting teacher, friend, or stranger who buoys us up with simple, yet sincere, kind words or deeds.

The bicyclist's kind comment to me was probably awkward for her to give because she had to ride so close for me to hear her, but she still did it. Her tiny passing compliment is something she probably doesn't even remember, but it is a kindness I won't ever forget. Even though I have never attempted a second race, in my daily race of life when I feel out of place, slow, or invisible to the masses, I remember her words: *You're cool.* And I am lifted again.

That bicyclist built the kingdom—a little piece for her, as I'm sure she felt royal for her efforts, and a huge piece for me. With the wrong clothes, the wrong hair, and the wrong attitude, I felt like a moat monster, but her tiny kindness dropped the drawbridge and allowed the royal feelings to enter me too.

In our own daily race, whether we run through the family room or the break room, we can always slow down to show kindness to another runner. It doesn't matter if the other runner is lagging behind or leading the pack; it is our duty to share kindness.

---

6 In Flaherty, Patrick, *The Scout Law—Quotes for Life* (Bettendorf, IA: Teckni-Corp), 49.

We princesses understand what it feels like to lag behind. We may appear to be keeping up with everyone else, but often, our hearts ache with hidden trials that put us behind. These trials stay unseen, hiding under the right clothes and the right hair. Because we have our own hidden trials and challenges, we know other runners, despite how right on they appear, also have trials. We know what it's like to feel out of place and a little self-conscious. We understand what it feels like to not come in first all of the time (or ever), and we know how it feels to be passed on all sides by people who seem better, more capable.

We also know how it feels when someone slows down in their race and leans over with a kindness just for us.

Maybe it is a compliment that keeps us going for two whole months.

Maybe it is a loaf of bread.

Maybe it is an e-mail just asking how we are.

President Spencer W. Kimball said, "So often, our acts of service consist of simple encouragement . . . but what glorious consequences can flow . . . from small but deliberate deeds!"[7] We know what these glorious consequences feel like. We've all felt them when we've wanted to bear hug a Beehive for offering to babysit when we didn't know how we were going to make it to ward temple night. We've felt them when we've wanted to high-five the woman with the overflowing shopping cart because she said we could cut in front of her at the grocery store checkout line because we had fewer items (and she didn't know we had an appointment). We've felt them when we've wanted to jump up and down because the bank teller told us she loved our jacket—the old one—and that our hair was cute.

And we can—no, we must—give those small kindnesses, those "glorious consequences" to others. It is our duty, even when we, ourselves, aren't shown kindnesses from anyone at all. Even if no other runner stops to be kind and offer us "glorious consequences," we can always, always stop to give those glorious consequences to someone else. We can *be* that person who shares compliments and kindnesses we may quickly forget, but they will be kindnesses accompanied with glorious consequences others may always remember.

We can be that person, and we must be that person. We covenanted at baptism that we *would* be that person. In Mosiah, Alma shares the promises we make when we agree to baptism. He said, "Behold, here are the waters of Mormon (for thus were they called) and now, as ye are desirous to come

---

7 Kimball, Spencer W., "Small Acts of Service," *Ensign*, Dec. 1974.

into the fold of God, and to be called his people, and are willing to bear one another's burdens, that they may be light; Yea, and are willing to mourn with those that mourn; yea, and comfort those that stand in need of comfort."[8]

Our baptismal covenants describe someone who is kind. Our covenants describe someone willing to build the kingdom of God on earth to remind others of their royal heritage. Our covenants describe someone who slows down in her daily race to help another runner along.

The race to eternal life isn't run at a sprinter's pace but at an endurance speed. Sometimes we go slowly. Other times, we go really slowly. But each time we stop to encourage another runner with every kindness we can spare, we show them a glimpse of God's kingdom and increase their motivation to stay in the race—that ends as we cross the finish line in happily ever after.

We can't help it if other runners don't slow down for us, but Elder Ulisses Soares of the presidency of the Seventy pleaded with us to be that person who offers a tiny taste of the kingdom as we slow down and are kind. He said, "Each one of us must look around and reach out to the sheep who are facing the same circumstances and lift them up and encourage them to proceed on the journey towards eternal life."[9]

We do not need magic to exercise our princess superpower. There is no formula we need to follow to show others the glorious consequences that come from extending a kind word or doing a kind deed. There is no special skill we need to possess. We just need to be kind. It is our duty as members of The Church of Jesus Christ of Latter-day Saints. It is our duty as daughters of the King. It is our duty as princesses.

Blessings to Bless

As princesses, being kind is our job, and Heavenly Father will help us accomplish it. Even though He blesses us with the *ability* to be kind, being kind is really up to us. We covenanted at baptism to mourn with those who mourn and comfort those who stand in need of comfort, and there is no gold star next to our name on the Church bulletin board if we're kind and no frowny face if we aren't.

Life is difficult for all of us, and I often think we forget our princess responsibilities and get caught up in ourselves and our own race. We become more concerned about our running shoes and running clothes. We want to

8 Mosiah 18:8–9.
9 Soares, Ulisses, "Feed My Sheep," *Ensign*, Nov. 2005.

keep up with the faster runners, not slow down to show kindness for fear of losing our place, and sometimes we fear that we don't know how to help others anyway.

We sometimes see our fast feet and sturdy shoes as gifts for ourselves. We accept our blessings and keep them, and we allow those blessings to lift us and help us run faster and better and more stylishly. We forget why we have healthy teeth (to smile) and why we have arms (to help) and why we have extra (to share).

I have difficulty in my own race too, and when I feel extra blessed, sometimes I just feel blessed! I forget my baptismal covenants to mourn with and comfort other runners. I sometimes think my blessings are just because Heavenly Father loves me extra for the moment, and I revel in it; I don't want to slow down to share my blessings.

At one such time of considerable blessings, I came across some strawberries at the grocery store on a Saturday afternoon. They were on sale for practically pennies, and I bought three two-pound cartons. It was more than my husband and I could eat, but I figured we would try anyway. We could have strawberry shortcake, strawberry pancakes, strawberry chicken, strawberry shakes, plain old strawberries . . . . Yum.

I knew every good gift (even strawberries on sale) "cometh of Christ,"[10] and I thanked Him profusely as I loaded them into my cart.

The next day after church, my family came over to our house for a visit. It was my husband's birthday, and we sang and ate blueberry cheesecake, my husband's favorite.

Afterward, as everyone was leaving, I overheard my sister Kat tell our mom that she needed some fresh fruit for Monday morning. I didn't catch the reason but heard the concern in my mom's response as she offered to give my sister fruit from her house. My sister hesitated, not wanting to drive out of her way to get home.

My heart was pricked, and my mind's eye saw the fresh, beautiful (and cheap) strawberries nesting in my refrigerator. I knew I should give my sister some of them—I actually knew I should give my sister *half* of them. My heart tweaked, and I knew that *this* was the reason I had found them in the first place, so I could give Kat half.

But I like strawberries. As a matter of fact, I *love* them. And if I gave Kat half of them, I'd have only half left! And I didn't want half. I wanted them all. Didn't Heavenly Father bless me with these strawberries? Wasn't

---

10 Moroni 10:18.

I important enough to get six pounds of strawberries? Why did I have to give up so much? Why is so much expected of me?

But I remembered the scripture, "Unto whom much is given much is required."[11] I had been given much—six pounds of strawberries, to be exact. And I knew that much was required of me.

Half.

But really, *half* of my berries? One carton was okay, but half would be one and a half cartons! Plus, *I* was the one who went to the store. *I* was the one who loaded them into my cart. *I* was the one who paid for them. Shouldn't *I* be the one who got the bigger half?

Of course.

Plus, to give her half, I'd have to get out some Tupperware and divide one of the cartons evenly to give her exactly half. And she probably wanted to get home quickly and didn't want to wash my Tupperware and give it back.

So I told Kat I had some strawberries for her, and she was *so* happy when I gave her a big carton of beautiful strawberries. It was ample for her little family of four. I, on the other hand, smiled as I thought of my two cartons of strawberries still in the fridge—definitely ample for my little family of two.

The next morning, my husband and I ate giant, juicy strawberries with our cereal. Delicious! They were every bit as yummy as they looked.

Later in the day, I took both cartons out to wash and slice them for some strawberry shortcakes I was planning to have after our family home evening that night. Even though I would use only some of them, I wanted to slice them all because it was easier for me to slice fruits and vegetables at one time and then use them when I wanted.

I got out the first carton that we had already eaten from for breakfast. I washed and sliced them into a bowl. They were beautiful! Then I opened the second carton—the carton I should have split evenly with Kat—and gagged.

The second carton was full of mold—not just a little, like, *Oh, I didn't notice those tiny white fluffies in the store*, but a lot, like, *How in the heck could I have missed those giant, green-and-black hairy globs?*

As I picked through the berries, I noticed that while many of them were covered in thick green-and-black mold, many of them were sound, whole, and perfect. They were giant and red and juicy and plump—they weren't even slightly squishy. There was no discoloration or even the tiniest hint of bruising. After sorting through the entire carton and putting the

---

11   D&C 82:3.

fuzzy berries in the garbage and the perfect berries in a bowl, I noticed that the moldy berries comprised exactly half of the carton.

Exactly.

I looked at the moldy berries in the garbage, and the Spirit touched my heart. I knew those berries were not for me. They never had been. I had bought them so I could share them. Had I given them to my sister like I was supposed to, they would have stayed ripe and whole for her.

They were no good for me.

I was ashamed. Alone in my kitchen, I felt embarrassed. I had been greedy with a blessing that was never mine to begin with. God had asked me to share what He had given me, and I had said no. He didn't ask me to give *all* of it, just half. And I had still said no.

I hung my head a little lower as I remembered a common statement I say in every prayer: *Please help me to hear the Spirit's whisperings so I can be the means through which others are blessed.*

Heavenly Father had heard my prayer and trusted me, and I had let Him down. And there I sat, looking at one full pound of strawberries, moldy in the garbage—a blessing that didn't have to go to waste had I only given them to my sister.

I told the Lord I would do anything and everything He asked me to do. But then I didn't. I felt like Peter, who promised the Savior he would defend Him to the end and would die for Him but still denied even knowing Jesus Christ three times.[12]

I think there are many who, if asked, would say they would die for the Savior. If asked, I would. Or would I? Maybe not if I wasn't even willing to give away half of my strawberries. We know that "inasmuch as ye have done it unto one of the least of these my brethren, ye have done it unto me."[13] The Savior asked me for my strawberries, and I said no—to *Him*.

We each have our own storage of beautiful berry blessings that Heavenly Father has given to us. They are blessings that help us run our race but also blessings we're required to slow down and share with our sisters and brothers who need a little kindness. We know these berry gifts—the money, time, resources, and knowledge—are only good for us to a certain degree. And we are obligated to share the rest.

We are all on this earth, struggling with the same issues that slow us down—health problems, family problems, money problems, and the list goes

12 Matt. 26:69–75.
13 Matt. 25:40.

on. If there is one problem we should never have, it is with other runners. We should never seek to have or become a problem for another brother or sister. Even if she's weird. Even if he's different. Even if they deserve it.

We are required to share our blessings with others and do what we can to build the kingdom of God through kindnesses extended. It is fulfilling our baptismal covenants. And as we seek opportunities to share what we have, we remind others that they matter to us and they matter to our Heavenly Father—and He will help us all feel royal.

Being Kind Is Showing Love to Others and to God

We are immeasurably indebted to our Heavenly Father and our Savior for continuously adding to our berry blessings. King Benjamin shared how we can never get on equal ground:

> All that he requires of you is to keep his commandments; and he has promised you that if ye would keep his commandments ye should prosper in the land; and he never doth vary from that which he hath said; therefore, if ye do keep his commandments he doth bless you and prosper you.
> And now, in the first place, he hath created you, and granted unto you your lives, for which ye are indebted unto him.
> And secondly, he doth require that ye should do as he hath commanded you; for which if ye do, he doth immediately bless you; and therefore he hath paid you. And ye are still indebted unto him, and are, and will be, forever and ever; therefore, of what have ye to boast?[14]

All God asks of us in return is to keep His commandments.

Commandments offer us the opportunity to show love for God, as He said in John, "If ye love me, keep my commandments."[15] And the greatest commandment of all is to love.

When Jesus Christ walked the earth, He was asked which was the greatest commandment. He answered, "Thou shalt love the Lord thy God with all thy heart, and with all thy soul, and with all thy mind." He then went on to share the second greatest commandment, "Thou shalt love thy neighbour as thyself."[16]

---

14 Mosiah 2:22–24.
15 John 14:15.
16 Matt. 22: 37–39.

We love God. When we look around and recognize the blessings He gives us, it is easy for us to love Him. Keeping His commandments gives us opportunities to show Him we love Him and also helps us show love and kindness to our neighbors . . . who are not as easy to love.

> Love thy neighbor—thy dog-barking, music-blaring, paper-stealing neighbor.
>
> Love thy other neighbor—thy early-mowing, non-waving, police-calling neighbor.
>
> Love thy cubicle neighbor—thy candy-thieving, constant-IM-ing, lazy neighbor.
>
> Love thy grocery neighbor—thy cart-bumping, non-caring, line-cutting neighbor.

It is often difficult to love our neighbors, especially when they don't appear to fit our definition of "lovable." However, President James E. Faust said, "We show our love for the Savior by doing the many small acts of faith, devotion, and kindness to others that define our character."[17] As we put forth an effort to show love for our neighbors of all types, we show love to God.

The two greatest commandments are intertwined but are also the result of keeping the other commandments. The Savior of the world went on to explain that "on these two commandments hang all the law and the prophets."[18] While these commandments are the two greatest, the rest of the Ten Commandments are in place to ensure that we really *do* follow these two great commandments.

- Commandment One: "Thou shalt have no other gods before me."
  Love God.
- Commandment Two: "Thou shalt not make unto thee any graven image."
  Love God some more.
- Commandment Three: "Thou shalt not take the name of the Lord thy God in vain."
  Love God even more.
- Commandment Four: "Remember the sabbath day, to keep it holy."
  Love God and go to church, where you can worship Him while you serve and love others.

---

17 Faust, James E., "Some Great Thing," *Ensign,* Nov. 2001.
18 Matt. 22:40.

- Commandment Five: "Honour thy father and thy mother."
  Love your parents. Love your Heavenly parents. Love your ancestors. This commandment comes with an immediate blessing: "Honour thy father and thy mother: that thy days may be long." Helping children understand this commandment will ensure that parents don't break commandment six.
- Commandment Six: "Thou shalt not kill."
  Show people you love them by not doing what you sometimes reeeeeeally, reeeeeeeally want to do. Especially when they don't keep Commandment Five.
- Commandment Seven: "Thou shalt not commit adultery."
  Love your spouse.
- Commandment Eight: "Thou shalt not steal."
  Love others, and don't take their stuff. Also, work hard for your own support and grow in love for yourself.
- Commandment Nine: "Thou shalt not bear false witness against thy neighbour."
  Show love for others by not making up lies about them or anyone else. No spreading lies. This commandment also has a lot do to with loving yourself and acting bigger.
- Commandment Ten: "Thou shalt not covet."
  Love yourself and the berries Heavenly Father has blessed you with. Love others and be happy for them. Love God and trust His wisdom in choosing whom to bless with your berries and how.[19]

Loving each other and our Heavenly Father is the duty of every princess. No matter how many berry blessings she has, every princess must share them with others. And when she does, she is not only showing them love but also showing love for Heavenly Father. Elder John H. Groberg of the Seventy said, "The more we obey God, the more we desire to help others. The more we help others, the more we love God and on and on."[20] As we spend every day keeping God's commandments and showing kindness and love to others to help and uplift them, Heavenly Father will reward us with a princess tiara—He has promised that if we keep His commandments continually, we shall receive "a crown of righteousness."[21]

Even on my worst hair days, when no fancy-schmancy, stone-studded embellishment adorns any part of me (not even bling-bum jeans), I have

19 Exodus 20:3–17.
20 Groberg, John H., "The Power of God's Love," *Ensign*, Nov. 2004.
21 D&C 25:15.

that royal feeling when I keep the commandments and show love to others by being kind to them.

As We Are Kind to Others, Heavenly Father Will Show Kindness to Us

I was recently driving on the freeway to speak at a conference two hours away from my home. I left with *exactly* enough time to get there—provided I didn't encounter slow traffic or get lost (I'd never been there before). I sped down the freeway with everyone else.

An hour into the drive, I passed an old red car stranded on the side of the freeway. The car's hood was propped open, and as I zoomed past, I could see a man in the driver's seat. His face was cradled in his hands.

I considered stopping. I mean, I knew that with my paralyzed body, I really couldn't help very much. Or at all. But I had my cell phone with me, so maybe I could call for help.

But I was in a rush. And surely *he* had a cell phone. Everyone did. Besides, I was already well past him.

But as I watched his red car shrink smaller in my rearview mirror, I heard the Holy Spirit whisper to me, "As you are kind to others, Heavenly Father will be kind to you."

My eyes widened as I considered my own self-perceived importance.

I asked myself a question: "Is this the kind of person I am—someone who passes another in need?"

I answered quickly in my mind, eased off the freeway, and slammed on the brake. I put my silver Baja in reverse and backed up . . . and backed up . . . and backed up some more until I finally made it back to that red car.

And you know what? He didn't need any help at all. His car was just overheating. It would be fine in a few minutes.

So I left.

As I thought about this experience, I realized that some might think I'd wasted my effort. Some might think I'd wasted my time. Some might think I'd wasted my gas. And *some* might think this man's car was this man's trouble. But no one else saw the smile of appreciation on this man's face when I offered a small kindness and he learned that, at least to me, he mattered.

I can't change a tire or even lift one. But as I change speeds and slow down in my own life's race to offer my abilities to others, it doesn't matter that I am so lacking and weak. I find that with minimal effort, I can lift *others*.

As I endeavor to lift others, Heavenly Father lifts me. As I show kindness to others, Heavenly Father shows kindness to me—kindness I need.

I stopped to help this man on Wednesday. That Saturday, I drove to Salt Lake City to speak at a luncheon for the Granddaughters of Brigham Young. I went early because I wanted to go to the temple before I spoke. I downed a cup of yogurt before I rushed out of the house, grabbing two string cheeses and a bag of miniature carrots for a later lunch.

Even though it was fairly early in the morning, it was very hot. As I pulled into the Conference Center parking garage, I noticed that my car was overheating. I was relieved to find a spot quickly, and I was sure that a few hours' rest for my car was just what it needed.

After a few hours, I traveled back to the Conference Center parking garage from the Lion House, where the Granddaughters of Brigham Young had met for their luncheon. They had given me a picture of Brigham Young with one of his quotes in a nice picture frame that made a solid table on my lap to carry my purse and the ice water they had given me. It was late afternoon and even hotter than it had been before. On my way back to the parking garage, I stopped several times to sip some water and eat my string cheese lunch. I was tired and anxious to get home.

I worried a little about my car because it was so hot, but I was relieved that the temperature gauge read normal as I drove out of the parking garage. I didn't dare turn on the cooler because I was afraid it might cause the car to overheat again.

I was a little hungry, having eaten only two string cheeses and a few carrots. I grabbed a few more carrots from the bag and sipped the water. I was glad to be going home to real food and an air conditioner.

My comfort was short-lived, however, and before I was even a couple of blocks away from the garage, my car overheated. I stopped at a stoplight, and the temperature gauge dropped again. Whew. I drove slowly forward, but the gauge needle zoomed up past the red H.

I didn't know what to do. I turned on the heater full blast and rolled down the windows. But nothing. I drove another block, hoping the needle would drop, but it didn't. I pulled over. I started to cry. I'd never been in a stranded car before. What was I supposed to do? I called my husband. He asked me if I was okay.

I looked around. "I guess so," I said.

He asked if I was hungry.

I should have been; I was before, but I wasn't anymore. I looked down at the bag of carrots. I was surprised that I wasn't. "No," I said.

"Do you have any water?" he asked.

I looked at the cup from the luncheon—yes!

My husband asked me if I was hot. I wasn't. I wasn't! I looked around—I had stopped in the only shade that existed in downtown Salt Lake City. I was right by a park. There was a slight breeze, enough to keep me cool.

My father-in-law had recently purchased AAA for me, and the tow truck was there in fifteen minutes. My sister-in-law lived nearby and came to pick me up. Her husband carried me to their car, and they drove me halfway home, where my husband picked me up and took me the rest of the way . . . and took me out to eat.

I am still in awe over how that day went down. My car drove me safely to Salt Lake so I could accomplish my errands. I was blessed miraculously with feeling physically filled. I had water. I was in a nice, shady spot, and even though it was expensive to repair my car, it wasn't a terrible ordeal.

I wonder how that day would have gone had I not stopped to help the man with the red car. I knew I couldn't do much except call someone, but as I showed him the kindness that I could, I was shown kindness when I needed it.

President Dieter F. Uchtdorf said, "The merciful will obtain mercy."[22] As I am kind to others, Heavenly Father shows kindness to me. As I care, He cares.

Once, in a parking lot (let's rephrase for some serious royal effect): *Once upon a time, in a parking lot far, far away, in the land of Salt Lake City*, I was trying to find a parking spot in an underground parking garage. It was crazy full, and the only reason the parking attendant let me into the lot in the first place was that I had a handicapped decal on my car. He wished me luck in finding an accessible spot.

I was optimistic and happy that he'd even let me in (everyone else was being turned away), but when I finally turned the corner into the garage, my eyes widened in surprise. There was no way I was going to find a spot in the garage. Not only were all the spots filled but the little roadway path that navigated through the multiple garage levels was jam-packed with cars also looking for a spot. They were inching through, driving up all of the levels of the garage and circling back down again in hopes that someone would exit and they could get their spot. I reluctantly joined the line of cars, and I wondered if I would even get my errand done so I could make it home before my husband got home from work.

---

22 Uchtdorf, Dieter F., "The Merciful Obtain Mercy," *Ensign*, May 2012, 77.

Probably not.

But I started circling the garage levels along with everyone else hoping to find something—anything! It didn't even need to be a handicapped spot (those were taken). I just wanted to get my errand completed so I could go home. I am sure that's what everyone else was thinking too.

As I drifted with the other cars at whopping speeds of two and three miles per hour, I noticed a lady in a white sedan up ahead trying to join the winding stream of cars, but to no avail. None of the cars would let her in, and they tailed each other closely to make sure she couldn't.

From my side angle, I could see her disappointed face each time she unsuccessfully tried to enter. She looked frazzled and tired, and my heart hurt for her. I slowed down a little to make room for her to enter.

What am I doing? I thought. I sped up. The natural man inside me reminded me that if I let her in front of me, she'd get the next parking spot and I wouldn't. I tailed the car in front of me so she couldn't get in.

As I drove slowly and closely behind the car in front of me, the inner princess emerged, and I shook my head. *What* am *I doing? This poor lady. Of course I will let her in front of me.* And I slowed down to open a space for her in front of me.

I smiled at her and waved as she smiled and waved at me and turned her car into the line. But as she did so, the natural man inside me flared again as I thought, *Oh no! What was I thinking? Now for sure I won't get the next spot! I'm going to be so late!*

The inner princess countered. *What does it even matter? So what if I'm late? I'm not going to remember what this errand was three days from now.* (And as I write, I really don't remember.)

Inner battles are so difficult because you are your own opponent; you're equally matched, and you can't outsmart yourself. But I ended the argument between my inner princess and my natural man. I decided that whatever else I did that day, I wanted to lie down in bed knowing I had behaved kindly. I said a prayer for the lady in the white car and asked that she find a parking spot and get to her errand on time. I felt good doing this tiny kindness. It felt good to overcome what came so naturally to me.

Even though that kindness was very small, Heavenly Father saw it. And because I was kind to someone else, He was kind to me.

As I slowly made my way along, a man walked in front of my car, between the lady in the white car (who I had let in front of me) and me, and got into his car. He was parked in such a way that his reverse lights shone on the face of the lady in the white car, who was too far along to get the spot! So I stopped, he reversed, and I parked!

Heavenly Father showed me kindness and made sure I was taken care of. Had I not let the lady in, I would have been one car ahead, not in position to take that spot. As we are kind to others and squash that natural man inside us—the natural man who wants to respond rudely to rudeness and indifferently to indifference and casually to casualness—we replace it with kindness, the princess superpower. God will remind us just whose daughters we are. He will treat us like princesses when we behave like them.

To behave like princesses, we must actively seek opportunities to be kind. We must use our princess superpowers to kill every quarrel with kindness. But in addition to actively seeking ways to be kind, we must be ready to act on extra assignments that we receive from our Heavenly Father through the Holy Spirit. We know when we can say kind things and do kind deeds, but only the Holy Spirit can whisper into our hearts additional, specific ways we can show kindness to others, ways we couldn't know by ourselves.

When I was a Young Women leader in my home ward, I was making a sack lunch for a combined Young Men/Young Women activity. We were going to Salt Lake City to visit Temple Square, and we each had to bring our own lunch. As I was making mine, I felt a tiny whispering from the Holy Spirit to bring an extra one.

I looked up in wonder—I mean, it was a strange request. But when it comes to following the promptings of the Holy Spirit, I have learned to act. There have been times I've wondered if promptings were really promptings or just me being paranoid, but I have learned that when it has come to obeying the voice of the Spirit, I would rather be wrong and do something good than be right and withhold my "berries" again and fail to help someone through their race.

And really, what was this impression going to cost me? A sandwich and an apple?

As I met the other leaders and youth at our church building, I talked with a father and son who were there. I learned that they didn't bring a lunch. The Spirit pricked my heart and told me that was why I had brought two. Not for me and someone else, but for this father and his son.

So I gave them my two lunches.

There wasn't enough time for me to return home to make myself another lunch—or even grab a granola bar or anything—so I called my sister-in-law

Paige, who lives in Salt Lake (the same one who picked me up after my car overheated) and explained what had happened. I asked Paige if she could hook me up with a lunch, which she did. I didn't even have to travel far to get it; she lived right along the way to the temple. I practically slowed down and opened my window, and she threw it into my car.

When I sat with the youth and opened my lunch, I saw that what my sister-in-law had packed for me was *twice* as good as the lunches I had packed. As we actively seek opportunities to be kind and obey spiritual promptings to be extraordinarily kind, Heavenly Father will bless us *twice* as much. As we work hard to build the kingdom and meet the needs of others through our kind acts and seek every opportunity to give them glorious consequences, Heavenly Father will do the same for us.

And through all of this, we are just being kind. And just being kind is all we have to be to merit kindness from our Heavenly Father. He will remind us just whose daughters we are. We will be reminded that we truly are His princesses.

Chapter 3
INDIVIDUAL WORTH

"I am of infinite worth with my own divine mission, which I will strive to fulfill."

(Young Women Personal Progress Book)

HAVE YOU EVER THOUGHT ABOUT what you're worth?

I mean, we hear that the "worth of souls is great,"[23] but *how* great? And how is this "great" measured?

The young women of the Church weekly recite the theme, listing the values they strive to live—faith, divine nature, individual worth . . . .

Faithful leaders help young women understand their individual worth in lessons and activities that hopefully help the young women understand what they are worth.

But how much exactly *is* our worth?

I know, I know: great.

But "great" is such an obscure measurement. I would love to see exactly what I'm worth. Quantify it! I need some hardcore numbers and calculations to properly assess my value.

If we add all of our assets (cash, house value, car value, jewelry value, etc.) and subtract our liabilities (mortgages, business debt, car debt, etc.), the resulting amount is our *net* worth.

In other words, if you died today and someone took everything you had and sold it, then paid off your debts, the amount left over would be your net worth. Our net worth is how much, according to the world, we are worth.

---

23 D&C 18:10.

I don't own my house; my husband does. His name is on my car too. But I think if I sold all of my clothes and jewelry and shoes and some kitchen appliances I got at my bridal shower, I'd probably rake in about $300.

A few hundred dollars really doesn't compete with people whose net worth we actually know. Usually, the only people who get this net worth number put to their names are rich people—very rich people. People like Bill Gates, who founded Microsoft and has a net worth of $67 billion, or Warren Buffet, the third richest man in the world, whose net worth is $54 billion.

Compared to these financially successful businessmen, my paltry three hundred bucks is pocket change. Depressing, I know. If I could combine my worth with my husband's, it'd add up to a little more; however, that's not allowed. Net worth is calculated individually. It is individual worth.

Giving it *that* title only makes it even more depressing. I mean, can you imagine a mutual activity on individual worth where you give young women calculators to determine what their worth is? Can you imagine young women with spreadsheets and pencils, calculating babysitting profits and shoe values? Can you imagine the sweet little sisters peeking over each other's shoulders to see who is worth what?

Young women with bling-bum jeans and highlights would tally up their totals and smile, while young women with holey socks and patched hand-me-downs would sulk into the corner to try to hide their low net-worth numbers and tearstained faces.

This scenario, of course, is ridiculous. Completely outlandish. Ludicrous. Or is it?

With or without a spreadsheet, young women (and not so young women) crunch the numbers. We assess each sister and add the value of her cute haircut to her Prada purse and matching shoes, add in the value of what she drives, and voila! Without even using a calculator, we sisters in Zion have become numerical geniuses, adding the numbers for every guest we see at a baby shower and every shopper in the grocery store. With every assessment and subtle judgment, with every comparison or appraisal, we put a value on each other and on ourselves. Seeing the value differences raises and drops our own confidence levels. We feel like less if their number is more, and we feel like more if their number is less. Net worth has become individual worth, which has become synonymous with self-esteem.

And we *must* have good self-esteem!

Not having good self-esteem is social suicide because self-esteem means we like what we see in the mirror. It means we're competent. It means we're confident.

Right?

Wrong. Self-esteem is Satan's creation to draw our attention away from our real individual worth. He does this by tricking us into believing we can increase our self-esteem (aka individual worth) by increasing our net worth. We increase our net worth with designer jeans and spray-on tans (sisters with high net worth have time and money for that kind of stuff, you know). Satan whispers that having the *right* hair and the *right* clothes and the *right* car increases our net worth, thus increasing our individual worth, thus increasing our self-esteem (we *must* have good self-esteem, remember).

Additionally, *not* having the right hair or the right clothes or the right car *decreases* our net worth, which decreases our individual worth, and subsequently our self-esteem. (Gasp!)

These are lies, however. In reality, the right hair, right clothes, or right car can neither increase nor decrease our individual worth.

It isn't possible to increase or decrease our individual worth because individual worth has nothing to do with self-esteem and even less to do with our net worth. Individual worth isn't self-esteem and isn't contingent on how someone *feels* about themselves. There is nothing anyone, no matter how many pairs of shoes they own, can do to change their individual worth. It is a set number.

And by "number," I mean a number so high it soars above Bill Gates's $67 billion and makes Warren Buffet's net worth of $54 billion seem like allowance money. Our worth—for each of us—is a number so high no one has ever counted to it.

Our net worth is $infinity.

The description of our individual worth is found in the Young Women Personal Progress book: "I am of infinite worth." Our individual worth, what we are worth on an individual basis, is infinite. This is our net worth value. This is what we are worth to God.

For a daughter of a King, one would assume our individual worth would be high. But as daughters of *the* King, our values soar. Our infinite value comes with a hefty inheritance. If we live worthily, we will receive *all* that the Father hath.[24] If we live worthily, when we finally close our mortal

---

24 See D&C 84:33–38.

stories, we will enter into our happily ever after, where we will receive eternal life, "the greatest of all the gifts of God."[25]

President Thomas S. Monson shared an experience he had listening to Paul C. Child, who "quoted from the Doctrine and Covenants, including section 18 concerning the worth of a soul." President Monson said that Brother Child "then turned to one elders quorum president and asked, 'What is the worth of a soul?'

"The stunned quorum president hesitated as he formulated his reply. I had a prayer in my heart that he would be able to answer the question. He finally responded, 'The worth of a soul is its capacity to become as God.'

"Brother Child closed his scriptures, walked solemnly and quietly up the aisle and back to the stand. As he passed by me, he said, 'A most profound reply.'"[26]

We have the potential to become as God is now. And we will reach this potential as we labor diligently in His vineyard, accomplishing His work here on earth. He trusts us to work hard, and He has given us much to do. As we live worthily of this eternal blessing, we will, at the end of this life and the start of the next, receive all that the Father hath, but we must understand what our value is to Him. Elder O. Vincent Haleck, of the Seventy, said, "If we are to prosper rather than perish, we must gain a vision of ourselves as the Savior sees us."[27] Our inheritance of all the Father hath is what we are worth. This is our individual worth. We are not just princesses because we think giving ourselves a cutesy title will make us feel special while on this earth. We are princesses because that is who we are: heirs to everything our Father, the King, has. His net worth is incalculable, and ours is just as "great."

We Matter to God

This grand inheritance is for each of us, and we don't even have to share it, which is a good thing, too, because scientists have estimated that the total number of people who have been born on this earth is 107,602,707,791. That is 107,602,707,791 spirits from heaven born here on earth in mortal bodies. And that's just *this* earth. From Moses's account, we learn that God created "worlds without number."[28] Just do the math: 107,602,707,791 x infinity = ...

---

25   D&C 14:7.

26   Monson, Thomas S., "Our Sacred Priesthood Trust," *Ensign*, May 2006.

27   Haleck, O. Vincent, "Having the Vision to Do," *Ensign*, May 2012, 101.

28   Moses 1:33.

I don't know either.

This number is unimaginably staggering, and I am truly glad I don't have to share my eternal inheritance with everyone else. (I suppose this makes me eternally greedy, but give me all of it!)

Aside from not wanting to share my eternal birthright, I don't really want to share my Heavenly Father's attention either. With so many here on earth and so many more on other worlds and so many more in heaven, I can't help but wonder how our Heavenly Father remembers everyone.

We know the worth of souls is great. We know if we live worthily, we will receive our eternal inheritance of all the Father has, but what I have a difficult time wrapping my mortal brain around is how Heavenly Father can keep track of His *billions* of children? If *each* soul on this earth (and off) is great to God, how can He make time for all of us?

How can He make time for me?

When I was a young teenager, I was pretty certain Heavenly Father had forgotten me. Even though He has said He sees every sparrow[29] and we're more important to Him than birds, I seriously doubted my importance.

I looked around at the sea of students cluttering the hallways in my junior high school, and I wondered how Heavenly Father could possibly remember me when He had so many others—just in my school!

I was sure I was lost to Him.

I decided to ask Heavenly Father if He was aware of me. I figured that if He was, He would tell me, and if He wasn't, my prayer would go unanswered, which would, in turn, also be the answer to my question.

I had already been scheduled to get my patriarchal blessing, and I thought that would be a good time to receive an answer.

Days before the blessing, I prayed more fervently, specifically asking if He loved and remembered me. I knew the patriarch would tell me Heavenly Father loved me—that phrase, I was sure, was in every blessing.

However, I knew that if Heavenly Father had heard my specific prayer and if it was really true that He loved me and was aware of me (one of 107,602,707,791 x infinity), He would tell the patriarch to say that *first*.

In the patriarch's home, he chatted with me for a short time before the blessing, and he asked if there was anything specific I would like to hear. I did not tell him what I wanted, afraid he would slip it in just because *he* knew it was true. So I told him I wanted to hear whatever Heavenly Father wanted to tell me.

---

29 Luke 12:6–7.

I sat in a hard kitchen chair, and he laid his hands on my head. I folded my arms and wiggled my toes in my church shoes. I was nervous.

There was silence before the patriarch spoke. With his hands heavy on my head, I started to worry. *What if I asked too much*, I thought. *What if I was seeking a sign and Heavenly Father is displeased with me? What if Heavenly Father wants me to have faith that He loves me? What if I have put a wedge between my Heavenly Father and me? What if the patriarch can't say anything at all?*

But the patriarch sliced through my thoughts and calmed me with a lifting peace that filled me from the top of my head to my not-so-wiggly toes as he spoke the first lines of my patriarchal blessing:

> My dear sister Margaret Alyson Hendleman, it is a privilege to use the Holy Melchizedek Priesthood and deliver our Father's blessing to one of his sweet and chosen daughters. He loves you and is mindful of you this day, and might I add, your Heavenly Mother expresses those same feelings.

I did not hear the rest of the blessing. My heart soared as my prayer was answered. I was loved and remembered by both of my Heavenly Parents.

Former Young Women General President Elaine S. Dalton asked, "Did you know that Heavenly Father knows you personally—by name?" She continued, sharing a message spoken by Elder Neal A. Maxwell: "'I testify to you that God has known you individually . . . for a long, long time (see D&C 93:23). He has loved you for a long, long time. He not only knows the names of all the stars (see Ps. 147:4; Isa. 40:26); He knows your names and all your heartaches and your joys!'"[30]

Because of this experience with my patriarchal blessing, I have never again doubted my great worth to God. He who notes the sparrow's fall knows me.

President Dieter F. Uchtdorf spoke about Moses's realization that man is nothing compared to our Heavenly Father. If we were to compare our net worth with God's, He would tip the scale with his worlds without number. Even Bill Gates would appear a poor beggar compared to Heavenly Father's infinite worlds. No matter how plump our wallets or meager our means, each of us on our own merit is worth less than the dust when compared to Heavenly Father. But President Uchtdorf goes on to explain our value in the sight of our Creator: "This is a paradox of man: compared to God, man is nothing; yet we are everything to God."[31]

30 Dalton, Elaine S., "He Knows You by Name," *Ensign*, May 2005.
31 Uchtdorf, Dieter F., "You Matter to Him," *Ensign*, Nov. 2011, 20.

We are everything to God, and our worth is great. If we live worthily, we will inherit everything He has, and He will make us rulers over his household. This is our value. This is our individual worth.

My Life Has a Plan

We are inherently royal, and we were sent here to prove ourselves worthy of our divine inheritance. We do this by laboring as faithful stewards in the Lord's vineyard during our time on earth, and when the day is done, the Lord of the vineyard will pay us the wages and give us the eternal inheritance we earn. If we worthily accomplish the work the Lord gives us, we will be servants who are worthy of our hire. "Blessed is that servant, whom his lord when he cometh shall find so doing."[32]

But what are we supposed to be found "so doing?" Not many (if any) of us have ever worked in a real vineyard or even grow grapes alongside our fences. The vineyard wherein we work is all around us. We till and toil to the best of our abilities to magnify our Church callings and strengthen our families and perform service for others. Our work is recognized by the Savior, the Lord of the vineyard, when we harvest the fruits of our labors in the form of strong families, well-executed callings, and services rendered, giving meaning to the scripture "by their fruits ye shall know them."[33]

Our duty is to harvest good fruit and labor as the Savior would labor. Elder Haleck said, "When we study the life of our Savior and His teachings, we see Him amongst the people teaching, praying, lifting, and healing. When we emulate Him and do the things we see Him do, we begin to see a vision of who we can become."[34]

Even though all of the laborers in the vineyard are united in growing grapes, they have different duties. Some till the soil, some plant the seeds, and some harvest the fruit. Likewise, members of the Church of Jesus Christ are united in the efforts of His vineyard and serve Him with all of our "heart, might, mind, and strength,"[35] and we do it in our individual duties.

Before we came to labor in God's vineyard, we lived with Him in the premortal existence, where we accepted our different duties. We were each given specific purposes to accomplish while we labored in the vineyard

---

32 Luke 12:43.
33 Matt. 7:20.
34 Haleck, O. Vincent, "Having the Vision to Do," *Ensign*, May 2012, 102.
35 D&C 4:2.

on earth. We are "of infinite worth," reads the Personal Progress manual, "with [our] own divine mission, which [we] will strive to fulfill."

At the first thought of missions, some of you might think, *Well, I didn't go on a mission. I'm just a wife. I'm just a mom. I'm just me.* Many consider their labor in God's vineyard unimportant and trivial. The assistant Nursery leader over snacks may feel her duty isn't as significant as the Young Women president, and the Sunday School teacher may feel inadequate next to the Relief Society first counselor, but Bishop H. Burke Peterson said, "One of the greatest challenges is to overcome the feeling that we are unimportant, that we are not special and unique. Do you think for a moment that Heavenly Father would have sent one of His children to this earth by accident, without the possibility of a significant work to perform?"[36]

The callings we have in the Church and in life are designed to allow us to use our talents—the tools God has given us to work in the vineyard—and strengthen our abilities so we can achieve our divine potential and become as the Savior is. Our work in the vineyard is not to hold the coolest, most technologically advanced tool and harvest the fruit closest to where the Savior stands, but rather, our work in the vineyard is to become *like* the Savior. All of our callings, challenges, trials, and blessings are the tools Heavenly Father gives us to enable us to work in the vineyard in such a way that we can become more like the Savior. Christ has said, "What manner of men ought ye to be? Verily I say unto you, even as I am."[37]

Heavenly Father knows us individually, and He knows what we need—what tools we need that will help us become more like the Savior. Heavenly Father must have discussed with us the significant work He has given us to do. To the ancient prophet Jeremiah, He said, "Before I formed thee in the belly I knew thee; and before thou camest forth out of the womb I sanctified thee, and I ordained thee a prophet unto the nations."[38]

Likewise, John the Baptist was foreordained to prepare the people for the Savior's mortal ministry.[39] Jesus Christ Himself was foreordained to carry out the Atonement.[40] "The doctrine of foreordination applies to all members of the Church, not just to the Savior and His prophets. Before the creation of the earth, faithful women were given certain responsibilities and faithful men were foreordained to certain priesthood duties. As people

---

36 Peterson, H. Burke, "Your Life Has a Purpose," *New Era*, May 1979.
37 3 Nephi 27:27.
38 Jeremiah 1:5.
39 Luke 1:13–17.
40 Revelation 13:8; see also 1 Peter 1:19–21.

prove themselves worthy, they will be given opportunities to fulfill the assignments they then received."[41]

The assignments we received before we came to earth are our individual missions. These missions are designed so we can assist others to become like Jesus Christ and, in helping others do so, to become more like Him ourselves. If we accept and do these missions on earth, we will succeed. If we choose to lounge about the vineyard, eating the fruit out of other people's baskets, refusing to dirty the tools Heavenly Father has given us, we can't become like the Savior and we won't be found "doing" when the Lord of the vineyard comes. We won't be worthy of the eternal inheritance that could have been ours. "Whosoever will save his life shall lose it: but whosoever will lose his life for my sake, the same shall save it."[42]

If we are laboring in the vineyard to keep the commandments and do what we have been asked to do by the Lord of the vineyard's prophets, we will gain more insight into the promises we made in the premortal existence, where we received our assignments.

President Joseph F. Smith observed that "through obedience, we often catch a spark from the awakened memories of the immortal soul, which lights up our whole being as with the glory of our former home."[43] I experienced one of these "sparks" when I was in the hospital after I broke my neck. I had a dream that I know wasn't a dream, but for lack of a better word, we will call it a dream. In this dream, I saw myself sitting at a table with a man. I knew I was looking at myself in the premortal existence before I was born. We were both wearing white. Between us on the table were papers, and I knew this man was explaining to me what it would be like to be paralyzed.

I watched as my spirit self exclaimed to him, "Oh, I am so excited!"

I know that each one of us had a similar experience in heaven, where we received our first lessons to prepare us for our specific duties we would get the opportunity to perform as we labored in the Lord's vineyard.

I don't know if I *asked* to be paralyzed. I don't know if Heavenly Father *asked me* to be paralyzed. All that matters is that I *knew* it would happen, I was *prepared* for it, and I was *excited* for it.

We were excited, and our excitement to serve the Lord must not wane because we have passed through the veil and forgotten our promises! Elder Neal A. Maxwell quoted Elder Orson Hyde, saying, "'We have forgotten! . . .

---

41   https://lds.org/study/topics/foreordination?lang=eng&query=foreordination.
42   Luke 9:24.
43   Smith, Joseph F., *Gospel Doctrine*, 5th ed. (Salt Lake City: Deseret Book, 1939), 14.

But our forgetfulness cannot alter the facts [*Journal of Discourses*, 7:315]."[44] The facts are that we are worth all the Father has, and as we discussed what missions would best help us reach our divine potential and become worthy of this ending wage, we told Him we would labor diligently in His vineyard on earth.

Laboring diligently, as mentioned earlier, means serving with our entire capacities to keep His commandments. It also means fulfilling the individual duties we promised to perform. We must discover what those duties are. President James E. Faust said that each of us came with a specific mission. "You can do something for another person that no one else ever born can do."[45] We must seek out what it is we were prepared to come to earth and do, and then, like Nephi's brother Jacob, after we have "obtained [our] errand" from the Lord, we must magnify it, "notwithstanding the greatness of the task."[46]

Identifying an earthly mission is never an "oh, that's nice" passive kind of thing. After we've been enlightened with a direction to travel, we must go that way.

The Savior can manage His vineyard all by Himself, but to reach our own potential and become as He is, He allows us to help and gives us the opportunity to be servants found *doing*. Heavenly Father gave us individual earthly missions to accomplish to help us achieve our potential. Elder Haleck said, "I bear you my witness of the Savior and His desire for us to return to Him. To do that, we must have the faith to do—to follow Him and become like Him."[47]

If we fail to identify and accomplish our specific purposes on earth, Heavenly Father will get things done. Without us. Bishop Peterson said, "Please don't make another have to take your place. He or she can't do it as well as you can. If you will let Him, I testify that our Father in Heaven will walk with you through the journey of life and inspire you to know your special purpose here."[48]

Our special purposes are not secret; they are waiting for us to discover and accomplish them. As we seek Heavenly Father's guidance, He will tell us what direction to travel so we can fulfill our earthly missions. To learn what our individualized missions are and what specifically we promised

44   In Maxwell, Neal A., "Premortality, a Glorious Reality," *Ensign*, Nov. 1985.

45   Faust, James E., "Instruments in the Hands of God," *Ensign*, Oct. 2005.

46   Jacob 1:17, 19; 2:10.

47   Haleck, O. Vincent, "Having the Vision to Do," *Ensign*, May 2012, 103.

48   Peterson, H. Burke, "Your Life Has a Purpose," *New Era*, May 1979.

to be found doing in the vineyard, "we must focus our vision on the Savior and His teachings . . . . The Savior has a great vision of who we can become."[49] The Lord of the vineyard is not a micromanager; He will not lean over our shoulders as we work or lounge to try to tell us how to better use the tool we're working with or where to weed. We must seek Him out to ask for His guidance.

And there is no line to speak with Him! If we look, He is simply waiting for us to ask Him questions about how we can better labor in His work so we can harvest more fruit and prosper. A handful of Sunday school answers shares how we can gain knowledge and understanding from our Savior: pray, read the scriptures, fast, and read our patriarchal blessings. As we seek His guidance through these basic actions, He will enlighten our minds and we will better see our importance as we labor.

We can also find the Savior in general conference. He has said, "Whether by mine own voice or by the voice of my servants, it is the same."[50] Every six months, I prepare to watch general conference by writing out questions I want the Lord to answer. The answers to these questions help me better understand my purposes. One of these questions is always, "What characteristic do I need to work on for the next six months?" I ask this each conference, and Heavenly Father always answers me.

During one general conference a few years ago, I eagerly watched, waiting to hear what characteristic I should work on. I became excited as one speaker listed numerous characteristics: mercy, friendship, trust, faith, bravery . . . but I didn't feel the Spirit tell me that any of those were *my* characteristic.

The next speaker shared a story and briefly described something as "temperate." I felt the Holy Ghost testify to my heart that this was the one I needed for myself.

Temperance.

Temperance?

What the heck was temperance? How was I going to increase in *that*?

Over the next few weeks, I considered just how I could become more temperate, whatever that meant. I right clicked it in a Word document and found synonyms: moderate, mild, pleasant, calm, self-controlled.

Hmm. Sounded good.

I thought hard about what I could do to get some temperance. I think a lot when I drive, and I drive a lot. Because I am so slow in my wheelchair

49 Haleck, O. Vincent, "Having the Vision to Do," *Ensign*, May 2012, 102.
50 D&C 1:38.

and in every other aspect of my life, I like the driving portion of my day to be the quickest possible, often exceeding the speed limit.

One day as I pondered while driving on the freeway, I had an epiphany. I could gain temperance in the *car* in my weekly hours of drive time if I committed to drive the speed limit!

I immediately pushed the breaks and slowed to 69 mph. The speed limit is sixty-five, but I thought that *for sure* I could never keep *that* commitment. I thought sixty-nine was slow enough.

As it turns out, my speedometer is off by four so my sixty-nine *is* sixty-five. But it doesn't matter because I slowed down to sixty-nine and never sped up again.

It is very hard for me to drive sixty-nine miles per hour. The hardest is when other people are driving slower than me (I never knew people actually drove that slow) and I want to pass them in the faster lanes but can't because the cars are moving too fast and I don't want to move out in front of a car that will have to slow down for me.

Ugh!

It is really, really hard sometimes. But the times that are really hard are when the temperance is growing. I don't increase in temperance if I'm blissfully cruising along at my 69 mph and enjoying the sunshine as I'm listening to my favorite music. No. The temperance only grows in the rain—when my wheelchair (that rides in the bed of the car) is getting wetter and wetter the longer I'm driving and the cars are whizzing past me. *That's* when the temperance grows. When it's hard.

I could tell I was becoming more self-controlled and temperate in my daily life, but the most telling experience happened during a pre-pageant event for the Ms. Wheelchair Utah Pageant.

There are three prepageant events, and before one of them, I was a little (lot) stressed. I went into the bathroom stall and prayed (I often pray in bathroom stalls and am so glad Heavenly Father hears me wherever I am). I told Him that more than anything, I wanted to be a good leader. I told Him there were many volunteers and many contestants and many contestant companions, and I wanted to be the very best leader I could be. I told Him I wanted to be temperate. I was afraid of snapping at the caterer or at one of the young women volunteers. I was afraid I would ruin someone's pageant experience by overreacting or showing my emotions when I was frustrated or distressed.

I told Heavenly Father I had been driving the speed limit for *this* purpose—so I could be temperate during *this* type of situation. I asked Him to bless me with the temperance I had earned during my months of driving the speed limit when it was hard or when I was late or when it was raining.

During the event, I surprised myself with the serenity with which I led and managed the volunteers. Halfway through, I had a brief meeting with the judges to begin the judging sessions for the contestants. Toward the close of our meeting, we heard a loud crash, followed by a shrieking scream.

The three judges and I were terrified, and one of them ran out of the room to help. She came back a few seconds later and explained that everything was okay. One of the young women volunteers had tipped over a food cart near the elevators. We were all relieved that it wasn't any of the contestants and that no one had been hurt. However, even though I didn't let it show to the judges, I was fuming. I couldn't believe one of the volunteers had been so careless.

I left the meeting to find out exactly what had happened and to verbally destroy the culprit. Why hadn't the young woman been more careful? Why did she have to *scream*? That was the worst part. A crash was okay and understandable but not a loud shriek that reverberated through the entire event.

I pushed my wheelchair toward the commotion where I knew they were cleaning up the cart and mess. I was going to give this young woman a piece of my mind for ruining the composure of our beautiful evening, and she would *never* behave poorly again.

But as I pushed down the hallway, I remembered how often I'd sat behind a slow car in the slow lane, wanting so badly to pass but knowing that if I did, I couldn't speed up enough and I would slow down the other cars. I remembered how often I had been late to a meeting but still refused to allow myself to drive faster than sixty-nine. I remembered how often I had felt as if I was crawling when other cars were flying by me.

I was feet away from the corner of the hallway, and I could hear the volunteers picking up the mess on the other side. It was the turning point, possibly the point of no return. I knew that if I rounded that corner, I would lose my ability to be temperate. Even if I didn't say anything with my mouth, my face would say it all. And this wasn't the time for me to speed. This was the time for me to turn around and drive the other way.

So I did.

And I never saw the commotion. I never saw which young woman had tipped the cart. I never saw who had screamed.

A couple of hours later, at the close of the event, one of the young woman leaders asked me if my full name was Grace.

"Um, no," I said. I smiled up at her, trying not to show how weird I thought her question was. Most people ask me if my full name is Megan (It isn't. My full name is Margaret, after my grandmother) but not Grace.

"Oh," she said. "I was sure your first name was Grace and that your middle name was Under Fire," she went on. "I just can't believe how calm you are! I would be going crazy with such a big undertaking and so many people and so many problems to solve!"

Growing in temperance has given me a finer skill to use as I labor in the vineyard. The Lord heard my request for additional training and told me what I could work on that would make me a more useful servant for Him. Every six months during conference, He gives me a new one (providing I have worked on the one from before).

Elder Neil L. Andersen of the Twelve shared how we can receive individualized messages from the Lord through the Holy Spirit during general conference: "As we have listened [to general conference addresses], praying for spiritual guidance, and as we study and pray about these messages . . . the Lord blesses us with customized direction through the gift of the Holy Ghost."[51]

This customized direction will guide us to develop talents and abilities and make preparations that will help us accomplish our earthly purposes. But we must *act* on the guidance we receive. Receiving guidance for increasing our effectiveness to labor is of little significance if we choose to not do what we have been told to do. We must act. We must be found doing. Elder Haleck has said, "As we put into action the teachings of our leaders, we gain a deeper understanding of our Savior's vision for us. . . . Study their teachings and ponder them in your hearts while seeking the Spirit of the Holy Ghost to help you catch a vision of these teachings in your life. With that vision, exercise your faith in acting upon their counsel."[52]

The Savior knows our individual worth, and He knows the value of our individual efforts to build His kingdom on the earth. Our eternal mission is to earn our wage at the end of the day and finally gain eternal life. We must complete our earthly purposes and learn how to best use the tools we have been given—tools that, when used well, will enable us to harvest the fruit whereby we will be known.

The tools we hold—our challenges, blessings, abilities, and trials—are specific tools to help us accomplish the specific missions we came to earth

51 Andersen, Neil L., "What Thinks Christ of Me?" *Ensign*, May 2012, 112.
52 Haleck, O. Vincent, "Having the Vision to Do," *Ensign*, May 2012, 102.

to do. When we seek for guidance from the Savior, He helps us refine our tools and tells us how we can better labor so we can better harvest. As we act on the promptings we receive and labor diligently, we will, when the Lord of the vineyard comes, be servants found doing.

Make Weak Things Strong

As we increase our abilities and grow as good laborers in the vineyard, we discover individual skill sets and unique purposes. These help us accomplish our missions, even in moments when they seem less appealing than others.

Initially, some seem hard and some tools seem dull. Sometimes we don't get the tools we want—we struggle financially, medically, socially, or otherwise. At other times we don't get to labor in the part of the vineyard we want to—our friends seem to all be laboring in the "mommy" section while we're stuck in the "can't have kids but must be nice while answering the incessant and inevitable question: When are you going to start a family?" section. Sometimes "we experience hard things in our lives that can sometimes diminish our vision and faith to do the things we should."[53]

My first Fourth of July parade after being paralyzed was miserable. It was my first holiday out of the hospital. I was weak, and the newness of this trial was severe. I remember sitting on the side of the road in my wheelchair as a Boy Scout troop came into view. They preceded the parade, and as they carried the country's flag, everyone along the parade route stood up.

Everyone, that is, except *me*.

And as I watched the flag go by, my heart sank. I put my floppy hand over my heart, but it didn't seem like enough. Tears fell as I realized I'd never stand for the flag—or anything else—ever again.

I was so upset that I made myself lightheaded. I doubled over onto my lifeless legs. With my head upside down, I looked at a butterfly pin my friend had clipped onto a strap that hung under my wheelchair. She had put it there so I would have something to look at when I got lightheaded. The butterfly pin was a beautiful silver with green and blue stones inlaid in the wings.

As I looked at it, I thought of the changes real butterflies go through— from creeping caterpillars, to suffocating cocoons, and finally to spreading their wings and flying freely.

I wondered if the caterpillar was ever tempted to stay in its cocoon. I wondered if it ever doubted its ability to fly. After all, it'd never flown before. How could it be sure?

---

53 Haleck, O. Vincent, "Having the Vision to Do," *Ensign*, May 2012, 102.

I wanted to wrap myself into a cocoon and hide. I didn't want to be paralyzed. I wondered how this change could ever be "freeing" like a butterfly's. But there was nothing I could do about it. The change for me had already happened. All that was left for me to do was spread my wings and fly. But I didn't think I could.

I *was* paralyzed, and I *felt* paralyzed.

Elder Cecil O. Samuelson Jr. explained, "It is this special blending of our common origins and characteristics and also of our unique attributes, experiences, and specialized challenges that makes each of us who and what we are."[54] And I was Heavenly Father's "special blend" of wheelchair girl and a lot of heart. I knew I had individual worth—a price paid by the Savior—and if I proved that I was worthy of my hire and worked hard in the vineyard with my unique skill set and specialized challenges to accomplish my individual mission, I would receive my eternal inheritance. And as much as I wanted to, I couldn't stay in a cocoon forever. I might have changed from standing to sitting, but I hadn't been fired from my duties and my mission.

As I thought of this, I quickly sat up—just in time to watch the flag round the corner and continue on. I realized then that standing *tall* was different from standing *up*.

Later that evening, I read a message from Heavenly Father in my scriptures, "I give unto men weakness that they may be humble; and my grace is sufficient for all men that humble themselves before me; for if they humble themselves before me, and have faith in me, then will I make weak things become strong unto them."[55]

I declared my independence on that Fourth of July. I told myself that not being able to stand was not going to stop me from *taking* a stand! I sat a little straighter, my shoulders rolled back a little farther, and my broken neck stretched a little taller. And I spread my wings.

Our mission calls to serve in this life may seem unappealing at first. But as we refuse the despair and accept the labor, we find new ways to spread our wings. And we find that with the help of the Savior, we can fly. President Gordon B. Hinckley said to the women of the Church that "the sky is the limit. You can be excellent in every way. You can be first class. There is no need for you to be a scrub. Respect yourself. Do not feel sorry for yourself. . . .

54 Samuelson, Cecil O., Jr., "Perilous Times," *Ensign*, Nov. 2004.
55 Ether 12:27.

"You are creatures of divinity; you are daughters of the Almighty. Limitless is your potential. Magnificent is your future, if you will take control of it. Do not let your lives drift in a fruitless and worthless manner."[56]

As we accept our missions, as unappealing as some may be, we will be servants worthy of our hire. We will be worthy to receive our eternal wage at the end of our day's labor as we find our purpose amid the pathos.

Finding Purpose in Pathos

While others might pity the frazzled mom, she finds her purpose in the vineyard as she teaches her children. While others might pity the childless wife, she finds purpose in being a good example of faith. While others might pity the single sister, she finds purpose in education and service.

In what others call "troubles," diligent laborers in the vineyard gain the footing to leap to triumphs.

Would anyone study the life of Helen Keller if she could hear and see? Would anyone read the *Diary of Anne Frank* if she had lived a peaceful, average life? Would anyone know of Mother Theresa if she were content to stay in her convent and pray? These are just three women whose lives had their fair share of tragic times. I am certain that they, like we, wondered how their teeny-tiny lives could affect anyone. I am sure their missions seemed long, ever so long and unnecessarily difficult. But it was because they found a mission call among the despair that their lives have affected so many.

Once a year, my family has a "cupcake cook-off" contest, where each of us brings our best cupcakes and we vote for the best entry. The winner gets a very ugly trophy and bragging rights. My family members take this contest very seriously, and we begin practice batches and smack talk *months* before the big event.

At our first annual cupcake-off, my husband, Whit, was severely disappointed. He was new to our family, and when we proposed the idea for the "cupcake-off," he undoubtedly had visions of mounds of chocolate-frosted, sprinkle-candied cupcakes. He was surprised, to say the least, when we arrived with our "normal" cupcakes in tow.

My sister, Kat, had dished homemade tapioca into little cups. My food-artisan mom had crafted tiny pie crusts filled with hollandaise sauce and three spears of short asparagus stocks standing in the middle, tied with

---

56 Hinckley, Gordon B., "Words of the Prophet: Daughters of the Almighty," *New Era*, Nov. 2003.

a red-pepper bow. A crafty niece and nephew made another contribution out of play dough.

Whit laughed—his laugh that he does when he thinks people are crazy (he laughs this laugh a lot around my family). "You can't call it a 'cupcake' cook-off if it's a one-serving-off!" he said. He never let it die all year, and whenever we went to my mom's for dinner, he'd ask if we were having asparagus cupcakes.

So the next year, the rules were a little more specific, and the entries were a little—sweeter. There were frosted chocolate-chip-bottom cupcakes, nutty caramel-swirled brownie cupcakes, ice cream–filled root beer cupcakes, and ginger cupcakes topped with whipping cream and chocolate candies, and a miniature second ginger cake (the ginger contributions were Mom's, and Whit said she definitely made up for the previous year).

I went for a strawberry-shortcake theme and made vanilla cakes filled with whipping cream and strawberries and drizzled with strawberry syrup.

We voted, and I won!

I was talking to Tom, my little brother, afterward and told him the strawberry syrup I had drizzled over my cupcakes had initially started out as strawberry jam. Whit had said he really liked homemade strawberry jam, so I tried to make some but ended up with really thick syrup—you couldn't even tell there were any strawberries to begin with.

I told Tom I was kind of embarrassed that I messed up something as simple as freezer jam, but it worked out all right because I used the extremely flavorful strawberry syrup to drizzle on the tops of my winning cupcakes. The next part of the conversation went like this:

Tom: And you used the syrup in the cupcakes?
Meg: Yeah, I drizzled it on the tops.
Tom: They're all pink. It looks like you did more than drizzle.
Meg: I had a lot of syrup.
Tom: So the syrup was supposed to be jam?
Meg: Yep.
Tom: So—you're telling me that you soaked the cupcakes in failure?
Pause.
Meg: Well, yeah, I guess so. But I won, didn't I?
Tom (in a voice akin to what you'd expect a wise old guru on a mountaintop to sound like): And so in failing, you succeed.

I thought it was pathetic that I'd failed so miserably at making strawberry freezer jam. It was truly sad—I mean, really, who fails at making something so simple? I was really hoping for yummy jars of jam to impress my husband, but I failed. I was pretty frustrated. I punched the oven and yelled at the berries for a minute. But I couldn't wallow. Had I moped around the house, lamenting my inability to make jam, I would have made a sad situation sadder.

After tasting the warm, melted freezer jam (apparently you're not supposed to cook it), I figured the thick, sweet goodness might come in handy later. So I put it in a quart jar and kept it in my fridge. I often looked at it, wondering when I'd use it, and then the upcoming cupcake cook-off came to mind, and I knew it was the perfect time.

Had I thrown it out, I might not have won. Winning the cupcake cook-off isn't a big deal (though my ubercompetitive family might disagree). But turning a trial into a triumph *is*. Finding purpose where pity might more easily surface is a big, big deal. Learning to use a tool we once thought was broken harvests the sweetest fruit.

Whatever berries make up your earthly blessings, Heavenly Father expects that even if we can't make jam, we will figure out how to make something else sweet. Even if we can't do and serve the way other vineyard laborers get to, we must figure out how to sweeten our service and realize how our special blend of attributes, characteristics, and challenges can accomplish our unique purpose.

While some moms enjoy their able-bodied children, others may be asked to struggle to lift theirs into and out of the wheelchair-accessible, always-breaking-down van. While some sisters hand out fancy bookmarks with quotes and cute embellishments when they teach Relief Society, others find it a struggle to even read the words in the lesson manual. When the meal sign-up sheet gets passed around, some feel embarrassed to not sign it, but they know that any spare time they have, if they get that luxury this week, needs to be spent strengthening their own families.

We wonder at times why we have such troubles. We wonder why blessings have been withheld from us. We wonder why the Lord would put us in such a poor spot of the vineyard when we could have been so successful in another. President Gordon B. Hinckley told the young women of the Church, "Never forget that you came to earth as a child of the divine Father, with something of divinity in your very makeup. The Lord did not send you here to fail."[57]

And we don't have to fail! We must succeed! Even if we fail at making freezer jam, we use the syrup to sweeten another part of our life and the

57 Hinckley, Gordon B., "Words of the Prophet: Daughters of the Almighty," *New Era*, Nov. 2003.

lives of others. We can take these jam-less berries and, instead of passing out pity-party invites, find purpose. Elder Haleck said that as we focus on emulating the Savior and serve as He did, we will become like Him. He said, "As they act on their vision to serve, they bless the lives of many and, in the process, change their own lives."[58]

Squire Bill Widener, from Widener's Valley, Virginia, stated that our part in life is to "do what you can, with what you've got, where you are."[59] Sometimes it seems that where we are in life doesn't hand us very much. But the happiest sisters are those who take the tools they've been given, refuse the pity, and find their purpose. God did not send us here to fail but to succeed, no matter what berries He gives us or what berries He takes from us. He wants us to find purpose.

When I came home from the hospital after being paralyzed, I was constantly reminded of my inadequacies and personal limitations. I couldn't walk anymore. I couldn't dance. I couldn't use my hands. Scars covered my legs, arms, and neck. My lung capacity was diminished, and I couldn't speak very loudly or even laugh. And from my wheelchair, I thought I had lost everything that had made me who I was. I remember sitting in front of a full-length mirror and looking at my ragdoll, disabled body in a wheelchair.

In a *wheelchair*.

This was never something I had thought would happen to me—I mean, ever. Before I was paralyzed, I was so far removed from the wheelchair community that I didn't even know somebody who knew somebody in a wheelchair. And there I sat—in a *wheelchair*.

Elder Ronald A. Rasband of the presidency of the Seventy said, "Some might ask when faced with such suffering, how could Almighty God let this happen? And then that seemingly inevitable question, why did this happen to me? Why must we experience disease and events that disable or call precious family members home early or extend their years in pain? Why the heartaches?

"At these moments we can turn to the great plan of happiness authored by our Heavenly Father. That plan, when presented in the pre-earth life, prompted us all to shout for joy. Put simply, this life is training for eternal exaltation, and that process means tests and trials. It has always been so, and no one is spared."[60]

---

58   Haleck, O. Vincent, "Having the Vision to Do," *Ensign*, May 2012, 101.
59   "Theodore Roosevelt," *Wikipedia*, Retrieved 04 May 2013, http://en.wikiquote.org/wiki/Theodore_Roosevelt.
60   Rasband, Ronald A., "Special Lessons," *Ensign*, May 2012.

It might appear as if others abound in perfect berries and perfect jam, but there is no one on this earth who has been given beautiful berries in every aspect of her life. There's an old saying that if someone's life looks perfect, we don't know them very well. We all—every sister in Zion—have stood (or sat) in front of a mirror and wept over blessings lost or never given.

Why is it that we can look into a mirror and see only the things that aren't there? Why is it that we wonder, like I wondered, how we are supposed to be useful on earth with such subpar berries? We wonder how we can make the jam we used to make or the jam everyone else seems proficient at making.

As I stared into my reflection, I started to cry. *I'll never be able to teach my kids how to dance*, I thought. Then I started to cry harder as I thought, *Well, maybe I'm not even going to* have *kids; maybe I can't.* Then I cried harder still as I considered my possible single future. *Maybe the reason I'll never have kids is that I'll never find a husband. Who would want to marry me?*

As I cried, I prayed. Having a testimony of the restored gospel makes it easy to blame Heavenly Father when things go wrong in our lives. We're taught from Primary that Heavenly Father *knows all things.*[61] He knows the beginning from the end, the front from the back, the inside from the out. And if He knows all things, surely He can *fix* all things. He can *change* all things. So why doesn't He sometimes?

I felt as if I had faithfully labored in the vineyard and the Lord had come and taken away my tools—then told me to work harder. Through heaving sobs, I cried, *Heavenly Father why have You done this to me? Why have You taken so much away from me?*

I cried for a long time.

But in the depths of my pity, Heavenly Father flashed a glimmer of purpose in front of me as He answered me through His Spirit: "Don't covet," He said. "I have given you more."

His answer startled me, and I stared into my reflection. I wondered how this could be more. I wondered how I could ever find more in the crippled mess that stared back at me in the mirror. I wondered how the Savior could see me as a successful laborer when my tools were broken. I wondered what "more" He saw.

More is difficult to see (mostly because it feels a lot like less) because it comes in the shape of burdens, hardships, and challenges. Many people feel that the more they have been given by Heavenly Father is more than

61 2 Nephi 9:20.

they can bear. They may feel it diminishes their purposes here in this life. They wonder how they, with physical, emotional, or mental flaws, could ever be useful to God to build up His kingdom on earth. But "trusting in God's will is central to our mortality. With faith in Him, we draw upon the power of Christ's Atonement at those times when questions abound and answers are few."[62]

Trusting in the more the Savior gives us is requisite for us to learn to use the new and often broken tools He gives us. We must "gain a vision of ourselves as the Savior sees us and as we act on that vision, our lives will be blessed in unexpected ways."[63] We can't wallow, staring at our own reflection and seeing only the less.

I once parked in an unfamiliar parking garage in downtown Salt Lake City. I had a meeting three floors up, and I was almost late, so I was hurrying.

I sped through the garage, found a place, and parked. Once in my wheelchair, I hustled for the elevator area—a small area with four elevators. But as I got close, I stopped. Blocking my way into the elevator area was a yellow-painted speed bump. (Maybe people at this business were so excited to go to work that they had elevator injuries caused by excessive pedestrian speed.) It wasn't a problem for most people, as pedestrians could use their feet to simply step over the bump; I, however, had to take this not-so-tiny speed bump head-on in my wheelchair.

The speed bump was tall and wide, so I knew I needed to move fast to get enough speed so when my front wheels hit the bump, I could use my arms to steady my wheelchair and let the momentum carry me over the rest of the way. Well, that was the plan . . . .

I underestimated the height of the bump and didn't have enough *oomph* to get my wheelchair over. Between the wheelchair and me, there was too much weight for my arms to push. So there I was in a practically vacant parking garage, high-centered on this ill-placed speed bump.

I couldn't go forward because I was too weak to push myself over, and I couldn't go backward—I needed to get to the elevator!

I waited a minute for someone to pass by and offer to help me. After all, I was a little girl in a wheelchair. Someone would help me, I was sure. So I waited. *And waited.* But no one came.

I got mad.

Where was everyone? Why was this speed bump here? What purpose does it serve? Why did I park here? Why was this happening to me? Agh!

---

62 Rasband, Ronald, "Special Lessons," *Ensign*, May 2012.
63 Haleck, O. Vincent, "Having the Vision to Do," *Ensign*, May 2012, 103.

But I couldn't stay mad at the speed bump forever. I had somewhere to be, and I needed to get over it. I had two choices: I could stay stuck on the speed bump, or I could muster my strength and get myself over it.

The decision seems like a no-brainer; obviously, I should work hard to get over this speed bump, right? But how often do we hit "bumps" in our roads and just sit there? Like when the Lord of the vineyard changes our duties, so instead of harvesting fruit, we are now pruning. Or when it's raining, He takes our tools and our gloves and our umbrella and tells us to weed.

Oftentimes when our duties are changed, we don't think we can go on—it seems too difficult. We just want all of the hard to go away. We wallow in our self-pity and misery and stay stuck, hoping others will see us and help us get over the bump in the road that we don't want to muster the strength to get over because it challenges us. Staying stuck is easier. Surely the Lord will realize we can do more for Him in easier circumstances.

Elder Marvin J. Ashton discussed our natural reactions to the *more* Heavenly Father gives us when he said, "We need not feel that we must forever be what we presently are. There is a tendency to think of change as the enemy. Many of us are suspect of change and will often fight and resist it before we have even discovered what the actual effects will be. When change is thought through carefully, it can produce the most rewarding and profound experiences in life."[64]

Our staying stuck, high-centered, and self-centered won't thwart the work in the vineyard. As mentioned before, God doesn't need us to help Him. He *lets* us help. And when He places speed bumps in our way, it isn't because He's trying to weigh us down. He is trying to build up our muscles for another, likely harder, duty ahead.

Maybe we're too weak socially, emotionally, or spiritually. Maybe we're confused or angry or hurt. Even as intangible as they are, feelings are heavy. If we let them, they keep us weighed down, stranded on the ever-present speed bumps of life. But no matter what feelings are weighing us down, the weight weakening us is our own. In the parking garage, stuck on this speed bump, the only thing keeping me down was me.

And when I realized that the only person I had to be as strong as was myself, I took a deep breath, closed my eyes, said a prayer, and pushed with everything I had until I was on the other side of the bump.

This speed bump was real—an actual yellow-painted bump guarding the elevators—but just as real was a stress speed bump I encountered on one extremely hectic and busy day. No one had died, and nothing had

64 Ashton, Marvin J., "Progress through Change," *Ensign*, Nov. 1979.

been lost. I was just busy. Really busy. And the stress was too much for me. I needed strength, so I went to the temple to find something that would help lift me over the bump.

I went with a prayer in my heart that I would receive the strength I sought. I kept my eyes wide as I looked for my answer anywhere and everywhere—in the foyer, in the hallways, even in the locker room. In the locker room, I stopped by a painting that intrigued me. I'd often passed by this same painting and hadn't ever really taken notice of it, but that day, there was something about it that kept my eyes locked on it for several minutes.

It was a painting of Jesus Christ. He was sitting down, and on one side of Him stood a young boy. On the other side of Him, a younger boy knelt and had his arms folded and head bowed on Jesus's lap. A woman knelt on the other side of the boy who was kneeling.

In what the artist likely thought was a reverent pose, the woman had her head bowed and her hand over her heart. She appeared to be looking directly at her own hand, and her head was bowed down and away from the Savior—she appeared to be leaning away from the halo of light that emanated from Him. She seemed sad, and she bugged me.

Lady, I thought, *just look up. The Savior is right next to you; just look up.*
She didn't move.
Do it! I said. *I know you can do it. Just lift your head like this.*
I demonstrated for her.
Here, just do like me. Lift your head. You'll see Him! Just lift your head and look up!
Still nothing.
Ok, don't lift your head, but just reach out.
I stretched my hand out to show her.
He's right there! Just reach out, and you'll touch Him!
This woman was driving me crazy. She just knelt there, looking down at her own hand and her own self while the Savior was within touching distance. *Please*, I cried in my heart, *all you have to do is look up! Just look up!*

My frustration with this woman was surreal. I couldn't believe she was kneeling there, looking down at herself, when Jesus Christ was *right there.* Apparently, that wasn't all that was unbelievable in the women's locker room. As I shook my head in disbelief at this woman, I noticed several temple patrons and temple workers on either side of me. The concern on their faces made it clear that my silent argument and demonstrations had caused a stir.

After explaining that I was okay and convincing them to not stay with me to help, I looked up at the picture again. Then it occurred to me that I was having an argument with a woman who was made of paint. She was not going to move. I took one last look at the sad painted woman who chose to look down at herself instead of up into the Light. My heart twisted for her one more time. And then I had a realization: *that woman was me.*

I was the one looking down at myself, even with the Savior right next to me. I was the one who wouldn't reach out for Him, even though He was within touching distance. I was the one who refused to look up. *I* was the one who was keeping me down.

I knew I had found the answer I had come to the temple to find. My own feelings of sadness, stress, frustration, and fatigue (no matter the cause) overwhelmed me only because I was acting like that woman in the painting—I was looking down at myself, my stressors, my sadness, my, me, and mine . . . instead of looking up, away from myself, and toward the Savior.

When I look down at myself, I don't see that much: just paralyzed legs and a wheelchair. My more isn't much to brag about. But when I look up, I find my Savior. And He makes up where I lack. He is strong enough to lift me over the speed bumps.

General conference was that weekend, and my heart sang as Elder Carl B. Cook of the Seventy shared his experience of when he was feeling burdened, overwhelmed, and stressed. On an elevator, he was staring down at his shoes when President Monson entered, "smiled and lovingly suggested, while pointing heavenward, 'It is better to look up!'"[65]

Heavenly Father had seen me (and my argument with a woman in a painting) and had offered a second witness in Elder Cook, telling me—and all of us—that while sadness, stress, frustrations, and fatigue keep us down, we mustn't stay high-centered on the speed bumps of life. We must look up and away from ourselves to see just how close the Savior is and that He will help us if we let Him.

The Savior has promised, "I will be on your right hand and on your left, and my Spirit shall be in your hearts, and mine angels round about you, to

---

65 Cook, Carl B., "It's Better to Look Up," *Ensign*, Nov. 2011, 33.

bear you up."[66] He sees the more in us that we struggle to see. He knows how to use the tools we think are broken.

Elder Russell M. Nelson quoted President Gordon B. Hinckley's means of overcoming obstacles in his life: "'I don't know how to get anything done except getting on my knees and pleading for help and then getting on my feet and going to work.'"[67] As I look up to find my Savior and push with everything I have, I get over the bumps.

We can trust that whatever bumps He sets in our way and whatever work He asks us to do will result in a sweetness impossible to achieve any other way. As we trust the Lord and willfully submit to whatever He gives us, we will, on the other side of awful, realize our trials never hindered our earthly purposes; they began them. And as we look up, we will find our Savior, who will help us over the bumps toward eternal life, where we will turn around and smile, knowing our growth and the growth we caused in others resulted from the difficult bumps we encountered in the vineyard. It is like the poem Elder Maxwell shared:

> My life is but a weaving
> Between my Lord and me;
> I cannot choose the colors
> He worketh steadily.
>
> Ofttimes He weaveth sorrow
> And I in foolish pride,
> Forget that He seeth the upper,
> And I the under side.
>
> Not till the loom is silent
> And the shuttles cease to fly,
> Shall God unroll the canvas
> And explain the reason why.
>
> The dark threads are as needful
> In the Weaver's skillful hand,
> As the threads of gold and silver
> In the pattern He has planned.[68]

---

66 D&C 84:88.
67 Nelson, Russell M., "Spiritual Capacity," *Ensign*, Nov. 1997.
68 *Sourcebook of Poetry*, comp. Al Bryant, (Grand Rapids, Mich.: Zondervan Publishing House, 1968), 664; in Maxwell, Neal A., "Premortality: A Glorious Reality," *Ensign*, Nov. 1985.

The pattern He has planned is a beautiful earthly experience for each of us. He watches our labors in the vineyard and helps us when we ask. We must look up to Him and allow Him to lift us over the bumps so we can find purpose in our "more" as we build His kingdom. And as we do, we are fulfilling our individual missions and will soon claim the eternal inheritance reserved for those found doing in this life.

We Must See the Individual Worth of Others

Our fellow brothers and sisters surround us in this life. Like us, they have individual worth and have been promised all the Father has. They each have their own individualized "more" in the form of unique skills and challenges and blessings. They each have encountered the speed bumps of life. They each are loved by our Heavenly Father, and He wants them back.

Each of them.

But many have forgotten their individual worth. They feel as if self-esteem is even too much to ask for, let alone "worth." They add the net worth of others and come up short when they add up their own. They wonder why God sent them down here with broken tools, and they look at themselves in the mirror, seeing mostly what feels like and looks like less.

Some of these brothers and sisters of ours hold the cardboard signs at the intersections. Some sleep in bunk beds at the women's shelter. Some see themselves as worthless.

I was asked to present a Sunday-night fireside at a juvenile detention center for young convicted felons fourteen to seventeen years old. I had never before spoken at such a facility or for that type of group. I didn't know much about them other than they had committed serious crimes and they were there long term.

Even though some were not members of the Church, all of the inmates could choose to attend this fireside. Most chose to come because it meant they did not have to stay in their cold, lonely cells.

I didn't know what I, a regular Church speaker who spoke at regular Church firesides, could say to a group of young, hardened criminals who had likely known little more than their life of crime.

This event was no "youth conference" with excited young men and young women wearing matching T-shirts and laughing and giggling together. The man who coordinated the fireside told me that gun-wielding officers would march the inmates into the empty, cement-bricked, white room, where they would sit, likely stone-faced, for my presentation.

With knots in my stomach long before the eventful day, I pondered what I should say to these troubled (to put it lightly) youth.

Would I tell them they should have faith? Could I tell them about the blessings of service to others? Should I share the youth theme? I spent many hours considering what I should do for this fireside—a fireside with an audience of nonmember youth who were only there to escape their prison cells. I wanted to know what I could share that would help them escape their spiritual prisons. What could I say to free their hearts? What could I say to help them—at all?

In answer to my fervent pondering, I felt the Holy Spirit put knowledge into my heart. I knew I needed to tell them about their individual worth.

I arrived at the jail and was escorted through several locked doors into a cold cinder-block room. I watched through plexiglass windows as the prison guards lined the youth up and marched them in single file down the hall.

My heart twisted as I noticed how young they were—for some reason, *knowing* they were fourteen to seventeen years old was different from *seeing* that they were fourteen to seventeen years old. I wondered how someone so young could have been so heavily involved in such terrible illegal activity that it had landed them in prison.

As they marched past me, I looked at their faces. Their beautiful faces showed just how hard this life had been on them. Some of them tried to mask their sadness by walking tall and tough—a show only for themselves.

I doubted the message I'd prepared, and I doubted my ability to reach them. What did I, a girl in a wheelchair who gave speeches and taught seminary, have in common with these kids? What did I know about their lives? How could they understand mine? We couldn't be more different.

The Savior knew my thoughts, and I felt a message from the Spirit once again. He confirmed to my heart the message I should share and what I had in common with these beautiful criminals. Once again, He whispered, "Tell them about their individual worth."

I was to tell them their value as sons and daughters of God. I was to tell them their infinite worth and potential to become like Him. I was to share that their individual challenges were not stumbling blocks but springboards to more that they could potentially be doing as laborers in the vineyard.

I prayed that I would be able to convey this message. I prayed that I would be able to see these youth as Heavenly Father saw them. I prayed that I'd be able to have at least a portion of the love He had for them.

My prayer was heard. My eyes were opened to a new realm, and I looked over the youth with new eyes, as if we had all entered a different room. The guards no longer bothered me. I no longer noticed the huge locking doors. I saw past the gray state-issue sweats and orange shoes and looked deeply into the eyes of my beautiful brothers and sisters.

These youth were worth everything the Father had. It didn't matter that they wore prison clothing at the time; someday their mortal would put on the robes of immortality. God knew them. He loved them. President Uchtdorf said, "The pure love of Christ can remove the scales of resentment and wrath from our eyes, allowing us to see others the way our Heavenly Father sees us: as flawed and imperfect mortals who have potential and worth far beyond our capacity to imagine. Because God loves us so much, we too must love and forgive each other."[69]

As I prayed for the pure love of Christ, the scales of resentment and wrath were removed. And I saw them. I saw beautiful, imperfect mortals who were worth just as much as I was—everything our Father, the King, had. I was able to see them as laborers in the vineyard who had just been given a different set of tools from me. These youth did not have to keep melting their berry blessings just because they couldn't make the same kind of jam as everyone else; they just needed to know there was a way to make something sweet from what they'd been given.

Once I was able to see past the immediate circumstances with eternal eyes, I was unable to return. As I spoke about individual worth and how it is our divine capacity to become as God, the hardened faces on my eternal brothers and sisters softened. As I discussed our individual circumstances and the "more" we're given so we can accomplish specific life missions, they sat up straighter. Many who at first hid behind the heads of those who sat in front of them leaned to see me as I shared a message that seemed to spark a memory within them. They listened. Some cried. At the end of my message, and with permission from their guards, they hugged me.

These troubled youth were imprisoned, and not just by the holding cells. Satan would have them believe they were worth nothing. He would have them believe this life was all there was and God didn't really value them anyway. They, as products of their homes, or lack thereof, wondered how God could ever love them when He seemed to have given them nothing and promised them the same.

We, plush in suburbia, will likely never see the inside of a holding cell. However, despite our overabundance of blessings, there are many who, like the teenage prisoners, don't realize their eternal value and keep themselves imprisoned by self-esteem, chained to the idea that the right fashions, the

69 Uchtdorf, Dieter F., "The Merciful Obtain Mercy," *Ensign*, May 2012, 76.

right hair, the right diet will someday set them free. They futilely try to chip away these chains with rolled-up beauty magazines.

The prisoners of self-esteem surround us. In discussing with a bishop what he wanted me to address when I spoke to his ward, he expressed his deep concern for the members. He told me they didn't understand their individual worth, and it wasn't just with the youth. He said, "I think self-worth is the most important message they can hear. Our youth want to base their self-worth on their popularity or abilities. Our older members are not much different. Not that they want to be recognized or popular, but they want to be valuable and needed. I had a member who was a mission president and bishop come to me this week with a heavy heart. His hearing, sight, and ability to walk are greatly challenged, so he is unable to physically serve as he once could. He believed that diminished his value as a son of God."

This former mission president was not unlike many youth, young adults, or adults in our world today. Many see an incorrect correlation between their good looks and abilities and their individual worth. Many see *beautiful* and *able* in the same context they see *useful* and *valuable*. These people are confusing individual worth (self-worth) with self-esteem, mistakenly believing that youthful vibrancy or physical ability brings them to a higher level of individual worth. These are the same individuals who become depressed and believe they possess less individual worth if they're not as pretty or well dressed or connected to the right social scene as someone else. Or even worse, these are the people who consider their individual worth heightened when they themselves are elevated!

There is nothing we can do to increase our individual worth because, like I mentioned earlier, we can't add to infinity! What could we possibly accomplish on earth that would somehow qualify us to receive *more* than the Father's *everything*?

Any princess with a crumpled dollar bill knows that even though it might not go through the vending machine, it spends the same in the checkout line. No matter what "crumples" us in this life, when we check out of the vineyard and enter into the eternities, we are still worth that full dollar amount. And neither extreme, feeling down on ourselves for our inadequacies or feeling pleased with our adequacies, can increase or decrease our individual worth or the individual worth of others. Nothing we say or do will change the promises we made in the premortal existence to accomplish our specific purposes on earth. How lucky we are that the Lord lets us help Him in the vineyard and build His kingdom.

Those prisoners in the jail and those imprisoned with the chains of self-worth misconceptions are not valued any less to our Father, and we must see them—all of them—with the same eyes of eternity with which He sees them. Elder Haleck said, "Just as the Savior saw great potential in His early disciples, He also sees the same in us. Let us see ourselves as the Savior sees us."[70]

When we pray for the pure love of Christ to give us an eternal perspective, these eternal eyes allow us to see others as royal sons and daughters of God, worth everything He has and with their own individual purposes to fulfill. When we pray for this love and are blessed to see others in this way, we care less what they're wearing. We don't look at what kind of tools others are using. We don't assess what they do for a living. We don't think twice about whether we'll stop to help them load their groceries. We don't hesitate to smile at them. We don't let them feel, even for a second, that they are worth less than everything.

We love them more.

We understand them better.

We forgive them freely.

And when we show others that we see their individual worth, we remind ourselves of our own worth. We remind ourselves that we, like them, are worth everything the Father has. We just want to become like Him. We want to be the princesses who, when the Lord of the vineyard comes again, are found doing.

---

70 Haleck, Vincent O., "Having the Vision to Do," *Ensign*, May 2012, 103.

Chapter 4
SING

The Savior is just a song away.

SHOW ME A PRINCESS WHO doesn't sing, and I'll show you a movie that will never be a box-office smash. Princesses sing. It's that simple. And every pink-laced six-year-old knows it.

Princesses don't sing because every scene in their happily-ever-after movie warrants such cheery behavior but rather because each scene doesn't.

Our lives are much the same. Who do you know who feels cheery as she looks at her to-do list that is ever so long? There are few of us princesses who believe we are capable of doing all that needs doing. We are each stretched to find time, ability, and patience to accomplish all of our tasks. And when we run out of time, ability, or patience, we have a choice: we can throw in our dish towel and hope the dishes wash themselves (which they never do) so they don't start to stink, or we can push through.

My father-in-law, Warren Johnson (I call him JDad), shared a story with my husband and me about when he learned how to deal with truly stinky situations. He served a mission in Guatemala, and at one point, he and some other elders received a live turkey to eat. Their landlord's maid, Rosa, volunteered to prepare it for them. She took the squawking turkey into the kitchen, and JDad said that after the squawking stopped, there was a terrible stink. It was so bad that it filled the entire house with a thick stench. They knew it was the turkey, and they wondered how Rosa could still be in the kitchen with that stinky bird. Plugging their noses, they peeked in. What they saw baffled them: Rosa was sitting on a stool, plucking the turkey's feathers out one by one—and she was singing!

JDad thought it was a little weird that Rosa would be having so much fun ripping a stinking turkey apart—even to the point of singing—but the landlord explained the reason for her song: it was so she couldn't smell the stench.

Like Rosa, we all find ourselves face to face with stinky situations. Our heavenly palace is hidden from our mortal eyes, and from the moment we wake (with bedhead—*real* princesses surely don't get bedhead) to the moment we lie down again on our not-so-satin sheets, we are exhausted from our day of laborious activity (do *real* princesses know how to spell the word *laborious*?).

And our non-princess-esque duties don't come few. We daily write lengthy to-do lists, and none of our duties describe the perfect princess itinerary. There's nothing on our to-do list involving croquet, parasols, or nature walks—that is, unless we're retrieving our kid's toy golf club from the neighbor's tree with an umbrella . . . .

And with so many non-princess items on our daily lists, it is easy to become discouraged and forget our divinely royal heritage.

Even though no princess wants to mope about her castle feeling burdened and overwhelmed, there's no moat wide enough, no sword sharp enough, and no turret high enough to protect us from the stinky onslaught of stressors brought on by the basic, regular, inescapable duties of daily living. And even the prettiest princess can lose her cool.

Stinky situations happen to the best princesses with the most well-meaning to-do lists. We try to keep our cool. We really try! We can deal with individual trials, even ones like a flat tire. It would be annoying but not cool-breaking—unless it is a flat tire on the way to your kid's big game with half the team buckled in your Suburban, spilling Gatorade into the upholstery and causing a huge stink.

Circumstances like this one are not farfetched; I am not writing fiction. We spill stuff or others spill stuff. We run out of soap midshower. Try as we might, the duties on our to-do list are longer than our patience, and we find ourselves in such a stink that we're tempted to rip out our own feathers, I mean, hair.

Sometimes life just stinks.

People are mean. Lines are long. Tempers are short. Places are crowded. They never came. They always come. No one notices. Everyone notices. It is too cold. It isn't cold enough.

And even though we aren't shielded from the temporary disappoint-ments of life that seem to happen every day on every bullet item on our to-do list, we don't have to smell it. Ever. Like Rosa plucking her smelly, dead turkey, we can sit in the heat of the stink and seem to others to be idyllically unaware of the putrid odor that has everyone else turning up their noses.

We don't have to feel frustrated when frustration is warranted. We don't have to feel stressed when stress is understandable. We don't have to be scared when fear is justifiable. We don't have to bite the heads off our family members when we're just hungry for some peace and quiet.

Blissful, sweet, and happy are not the names of any small men in our royal lives, nor are they feelings reserved only for the cartoon fairytale princesses. They are for *us* as well, even in spite of all of the sleepy, bashful, dopey, and grumpy situations in which we find ourselves.

And all we have to do is sing.

Before she moved in with the dwarves, Snow White began her Disney movie debut singing for her prince to find her. We can take a tip from this fair-skinned princess and sing for our Savior—the Prince of Peace—to come find us.

Songs that bring the Savior relieve us from the stench when, for whatever reason, our to-do list begins to stink. The Savior will come *today* when we sing.

Snow White knew her prince would come and waited patiently until the movie was almost over. Even though her life stank and was full of troubles and stresses (new house, lots of chores, lonely neighborhood), she seemed happily unaware of her predicament as she sang through each scene. She, like Rosa, teaches us to keep our heads above the stench with song.

Elder Joseph B. Wirthlin quoted President Hinckley, who told us what we must do to live like princesses so we can reach our happily-ever-after destination: "'I invite every one of you,' he has said, 'wherever you may be as members of this church, to stand on your feet and with a song in your heart move forward, living the gospel, loving the Lord, and building the kingdom.'"[71]

Earlier, Elder Wirthlin stated, "In every age we are faced with a choice. We can trust in our own strength, or we can journey to higher ground and come unto Christ. Each choice has a consequence. Each consequence, a destination."[72]

The destination we seek is our happily ever after.

To bring the Lord closer, we must build His kingdom and love Him. I have never seen the heavens open to show me exactly what we are working

71 Wirthlin, Joseph B., "Journey to Higher Ground," *Ensign*, Nov. 2005.
72 Ibid.

toward, but if I ever get to, I am sure I will see and feel as Alma did when he said, "Yea, methought I saw . . . God sitting upon his throne, surrounded with numberless concourses of angels, in the attitude of singing and praising their God; yea, and my soul did long to be there."[73] Without even seeing the heavens open, *my* soul longs to be there. But I am here. *We* are here. And in this not-so-palatial place, when we have a song in our hearts, we are behaving royally and are fit for the kingdom we are building.

Having a song in our hearts keeps the Prince of Peace by our side and our hearts free from the stink our to-do lists might cause. Singing turns every princess's downhearted situation into a heart-hugging, heaven-kissed sensation so that when we do see the heavens open and God sitting upon His throne and hear the numberless angels singing, we will recognize the melody.

President Boyd K. Packer once quoted a wise man, who stated, "'Music is one of the most forceful instruments for governing the mind.'"[74] As we sing, we keep the Savior, the Prince of Peace, near us. It is like the song reads:

> Nearer, my God, to thee,
> Nearer to thee!
> E'en though it be a cross
> That raiseth me.
> Still all my song shall be
> Nearer, my God, to thee
> Nearer, my God, to thee,
> Nearer to thee![75]

We become nearer to God as we sing, not because we get to visit our heavenly home but because the Savior visits His kingdom on earth, reminding us of our divine heritage and royal birth.

We have been commanded to "pray always, that [we] may come off conqueror."[76] Practically every situation warrants prayer, but few situations make kneeling in prayer convenient.

Singing a song for the Savior is not a replacement for prayer; it is prayer. We know that "the song of the righteous is a prayer unto me, and it shall

---

73 Alma 36:22.
74 Packer, Boyd K., "Worthy Music, Worthy Thoughts," *New Era*, April 2008, 9.
75 Adams, Sarah F., "Nearer, My God, to Thee," *Hymns*, no. 100.
76 D&C 10:5.

be answered with a blessing upon their heads."[77] It is a prayer the Savior hears—a prayer we can pray all day, every day. When we sing our prayer to Him, He will rescue us from the stench and place His promised blessing upon our heads—a crown. A crown fit for a princess who is fit for the kingdom she is building.

Do Your Duties on Your To-Do List with a Heart Full of Song

After I accidentally jumped off the cliff, I was flown to a hospital in Salt Lake City. Numerous surgeries repaired my legs, arms, and neck, and I lay in shock trauma waiting for, well, I'm not exactly sure what. Shock trauma is where you go when the doctors aren't sure whether or not you're going to die. I suppose I was waiting for my body to stabilize enough to send me into an intensive care unit.

In the shock trauma ward, I was bandaged and bound and had swollen like a watermelon. I couldn't breathe without assistance. I had tubes going every which way. My left wrist was surgically repaired and fitted with an external fixator that looked like my arm had been attacked by rogue supplies from Home Depot. My neck was fused and stabilized with a metal halo, which was screwed into my head. I had a tube in my nose that fed me and tubes in my arms that watered me and gave me medicine and tubes in my chest that drained the bloody fluid that filled my lungs. I had a fat blue tube, not unlike a garden hose, that came out of my mouth and hooked to a breathing machine.

When I awoke, all I could see were lights above me, highlighting the tubes protruding from my face and body. I bit down on the tube in my mouth and tried to spit it out, but I couldn't. I tried to lift my arms to grab the tubes and pull them out but couldn't—they were tied to the bedrails. I found out later that because of the extensive physical damage that had occurred, the doctors were certain I had brain damage, so to stop me from pulling out the tubes, they tied my arms to the bed.

I didn't know where anyone was or why I was like this or even how long I had been there—I mean, I remembered falling off the cliff, but the time between that point and waking up was a blur.

I tried to yell for help but couldn't. I wanted someone, anyone, to be with me. I was scared. Really scared.

I had a clip of some kind on one of my fingers. I have since learned that it monitored my heartbeat, but at the time, I thought that maybe an alarm

77 D&C 25:12.

would sound if I could get it off. My fingers and hands were paralyzed, and because my arms were tied down, it took a lot of struggle to pull, push, and finally slide the clip off my finger.

A quiet, constant alarm sounded.

Yes! I thought. *Someone will for sure come tend to me and explain what is happening!* I kept my eyes glued to the open door.

But the quiet alarm sounded for five minutes.

Ten.

Fifteen.

No one came. The alarm was too quiet. And I remained alone—and lonely. And scared.

I remembered a visit I'd had with a branch president when I was in a singles ward in Orlando, Florida. I was at the age at which young single adults tend to go inactive, and to help me keep close to the Savior, he told me to keep a song in my heart—any song—that I could summon at a moment's notice. He said the quickest way to the Savior was through a song. He told me singing a song would help me resist temptation and stay close to the gospel.

After visiting with my branch president, the song I chose to keep filed away was "I Love to See the Temple." I sang it constantly, reminding myself of just *where* I was going (someday). And it did help me overcome temptation.

But as I lay on the hospital bed in shock trauma, the only temptation I had was to scream for help—and I couldn't. I resisted the panic that kept inching its way into my throat and eyes, though panicking seemed to be the most logical response to this situation. As I watched the door for someone to come in and be with me, I remembered my branch president's counsel to find the Savior through a song. I knew I needed to sing. This whole situation stank (to say the least), and I didn't know how long it would last (or how long it had already lasted). So before I realized I was paralyzed and before I realized I would be in a wheelchair for the rest of my mortal life and before "wheels" meant anything to me, I sang the first song that came to my mind:

> The world has need of willing men
> Who wear the worker's seal.
> Come, help the good work move along;
> Put your shoulder to the wheel.
> Put your shoulder to the wheel; push along,

Do your duty with a heart full of song,
We all have work; let no one shirk.
Put your shoulder to the wheel.[78]

My duty was to remain calm in that hospital bed—for my own sanity—
and not shirk . . . or shriek (or both) like I wanted to. Someone finally
came, but as I sang that song over and over in my heart for the duration of
my four-month hospital stay, I was able to manage myself calmly, even in
the thick of a stinky situation. I sang that song anytime I was frustrated or
scared. I never sang it aloud—I didn't have the physical ability to speak most
of the time, and when I finally could speak, I was too weak to sing—but my
silent song echoed loudly in heaven, and I know my song was heard.

In my first sacrament meeting back in my home ward, I sat in the
back, slumped over in my wheelchair. I lacked the strength to even sit
straight. My brother Tom held the hymnal toward me as the congregation
sang the opening song: "Put Your Shoulder to the Wheel."
Push along.
Do your duty with a heart full of song.
The Spirit flooded my heart. I knew the music I had never sung aloud
resounded in heaven's ears. The Prince of Peace comforted me through my
hospital stay and came again on my first Sunday back to remind me that
He heard me and will hear me when I seek Him through song. He gave
me a small tender mercy, an individualized blessing, a reminder that I am
the King's daughter and that the Prince of Peace will uphold me.

The song I sang in the hospital began to take on literal meaning when
I returned home. Being a daughter of the King in a wheelchair is awkward.
I am awkward. I am slow and even slower on carpet or up hills. I dodge
every bump, incline, pebble, or miniscule obstacle I can because they don't
feel very miniscule under the wheels.

As slow as I am now, I was even slower and more awkward at first. I had
never sat in a wheelchair before I was paralyzed, let alone attempted to push
one around. But coming home from the hospital in a wheelchair was surreal.
I was very uncomfortable as I tried to maneuver around the house or down
the sidewalk. I didn't understand how best to push, so at first, I used only the
very tops of the wheels and pushed them with short, staccato bursts.

One day, I took a "walk" with my dad around the block. I began to
notice that if I started with my hands farther back on the wheels and then
pushed forward farther, dropping my shoulders, I propelled the wheelchair,

---

78   Thompson, Will L., "Put Your Shoulder to the Wheel," *Hymns*, no. 252

and myself, farther faster. In essence, literally putting my "shoulder to the wheel" lengthened my stride.

I breathed a sigh of relief at this discovery. It doubled—tripled—the results of my effort. It made me more efficient. I put my shoulder to the wheel daily—literally and figuratively. All of us have our individual duties, but the same steps apply: we need to put our shoulders to the wheel and do our duty, whatever it is, with a heart full of song. Having a song in our heart will lengthen our stride. It will make us faster and more efficient as God's builders.

Elder Wirthlin shared what helped him push through fatigue:

> When I feel tired, I remember the words of the Prophet Joseph Smith:
>> "Shall we not go on in so great a cause? Go forward and not backward. Courage, brethren; and on, on to the victory! Let your hearts rejoice, and be exceedingly glad. Let the earth break forth into singing . . . .
>> "Let the woods and all the trees of the field praise the Lord; . . . and let all the sons of God shout for joy!"
>
> For you members of the Church who hold back because of feelings of inadequacy, I plead with you to step forward, put your shoulder to the wheel, and push. Even when you feel that your strength can add little, the Church needs you. The Lord needs you. Remember that the Lord often chooses "the weak things of the world" to accomplish His purposes.
>
> To all who are weary, let the comforting words of the Savior console you: "Come unto me, all ye that labour and are heavy laden, and I will give you rest." Let us rely on that promise. The power of God can infuse our spirits and bodies with energy and vigor. I urge you to seek this blessing from the Lord.[79]

We are the "weak things of the world." If we work with a heart full of song and seek the Savior through musical prayer, He will make "weak things become strong" to us.[80] By ourselves, we aren't strong enough to fight the stinky assault of every day. But with a heart full of song, the Prince of Peace

---

79 Wirthlin, Joseph B., "Concern for the One," *Ensign*, May 2008, 18–19.
80 Ether 12:27.

will come and plug our noses as we pluck our daily turkeys, freeing us from the stench.

Sing Away the Sad

When I was twenty, one very late night, a stinking turkey of an argument with a friend led to a 2:00 a.m. run. Before I was paralyzed, I took care of any anger or frustrations I felt by running. I wasn't a true runner and didn't do it for fun, but it was extremely useful for tiring me out so I wasn't angry anymore. The late night (or early morning) didn't matter to me, and I tied on my shoes and ran out the door.

My family had recently moved into a new, small town, and I wasn't familiar with the neighborhood, so I ran until I got lost (which didn't take too long). I didn't recognize where I was, but I didn't care. I was tired, and after a good hard run, I felt better. I clasped my hands on top of my head and cooled down as I walked toward the only light on the street, which lit up the entrance of an LDS Church building. I sat on the cement steps near the glass doors. I had run off all the grumpiness, and there was a quiet stillness inside me and surrounding me.

As I sat there in the stillness on those cool cement steps, I heard singing. I heard a choir from inside the chapel sing "I Know That My Redeemer Lives." I stood, walked to the glass doors, and peered in. Part of me wondered what a choir was doing in the chapel in the middle of the night, and part of me knew I was not hearing the music with my mortal ears.

Inside the building, it was dark. I could see no lights anywhere, but the singing continued.

> What comfort this sweet sentence gives!
> He lives, he lives, who once was dead.
> He lives, my ever-living Head.[81]

I stared into the dark building, unable to see anything but empty hallways. I put my ear on the door. Even though the music didn't get any louder, I knew it was coming from inside. I stood there in the light of the street lamp, leaning my entire body onto the glass door. I wanted to be with the music. The night was quiet, but my heart sang each verse loud. No grand throne room could have felt more royal than the empty doorway of that deserted chapel. The music reminded me that my Prince, the Prince of Peace, was not far, just a song away.

---

81 Medley, Samuel, "I Know That My Redeemer Lives," *Hymns*, no. 136.

My storybook doesn't have to be in its final chapter for Him to come rescue me from stinky situations. I know Heavenly Father cares. He cared enough to send His angels to sing to me about His Son, reminding me where happiness comes from, reminding me I can be happy through every page of my life.

Happiness is not a goal; it is a way of being. You don't have to be beyond your trials to be happy. As we begin some of our life's chapters with phrases like, "She never knew it was coming . . . ." or, "Her worst fears were realized when . . ." we can have happiness right along with every gloomy introduction that might describe our lives. Happiness is for each of us in every chapter. It comes as we find the Savior, and we easily find Him through songs.

I love to sing to find my Savior, though I am not a singer. Being paralyzed limited my body, but the ensuing lung damage substantially limited my breathing capacity. I can no longer laugh, at least not like I used to. After I was paralyzed, my laugh made absolutely no noise. I just shook slightly. When I laughed, it was hard to keep myself upright. Because laughing made me fall forward in my chair and shake, people often thought I was having a seizure. Needless to say, it was awkward. I didn't like to laugh anymore.

As the years went by, my lung capacity slightly strengthened, and I could eventually speak more loudly and for longer periods. But my laugh didn't return.

After being paralyzed for more than seven years, I wondered if I would ever hear my own laugh again on this earth. Every time I laughed with my family or my husband's family, I couldn't hear myself. It made me sad.

One night in prayer, I asked Heavenly Father what I could do, if anything, to regain my ability to laugh. I told Him I didn't know if this was a very important request because it was such a small thing, but in the morning, as I silently did the laundry (I ponder as I do chores—it's a princess thing), I received my answer, letting me know that the things that were important to me were important to Him.

Through His Spirit, He told me that if I wanted to regain the ability to laugh again, I had to sing—at the top of my voice every day. So I began to sing (terribly off key and fainting every so often because of the difficulty), and now, a couple of years later, I can hear my laugh—just barely. I need a little more singing time before I get my full laugh back, but truly, it is coming.

Losing one's ability to laugh is not a trial only for the respiratory compromised. Even if you have never lost your ability to breathe, you have, at one time or other, lost your ability to laugh. I know because no princess, no matter how cute her giggle is, feels like laughing when her carriage gets a flat tire. No princess, no matter how carefree she is, feels like laughing when the power goes out and her dinner's halfway cooked and her kids are hungry. No princess, no matter how knee-slappingly funny her prince is, feels like laughing when he leaves his knightly socks on the floor *next* to the clothes hamper (again). And with or without lung damage, laughter damage happens . . . to even the best princesses.

But laughter damage is avoidable and repairable through song—but not just any song. In my personal research, I have tried many songs to brighten my mood and keep my laugh ready, but the only songs that truly wipe away my tears and calm my troubled heart are the songs that lift my voice to the Savior. No other song, no matter how happy the beat or clever the words, works as quickly and as thoroughly as a song that praises the Prince of Peace, who is the source of happiness.

I made meatball sandwiches for lunch one afternoon. My husband and I were eating together, and I was cutting mine with a fork (I don't like to hold goopy food). In my cutting, I slid the plate too close to the edge of the table and accidentally flipped the entire thing over and onto my lap—splashing red marinara all over my favorite white dress.

Grr.

I was speaking later that evening and had to wear a dress, so I changed into a different one and began my afternoon work. A short time later, I was back in the kitchen making dinner. I put on an apron and tied it tightly so I wouldn't have to change again. I put my big red cutting board on my lap because it acted like a little counter so I could easily reach stuff. I was making baked chicken, so I put the casserole dish with raw chicken and seasonings on my lap too. I was rubbing some seasonings and butter on the chicken when I accidentally flipped the entire casserole dish off my lap, sending chicken, butter, seasonings, and the cutting board crashing onto the floor.

I froze. With huge, I-can't-believe-this eyes, I stared. My can't-believe-this eyes started to water, and I felt a lump in my throat. My lip quivered, and I knew I was about to lose my cool. But before my emotions could catch up to my tear ducts, I made my mouth sing:

> When upon life's billows you are tempest-tossed,
> When you are discouraged, thinking all is lost.[82]

---

82 Oatman, Johnson, Jr., "Count Your Blessings," *Hymns*, no. 241.

That's as far as I got. My tears subsided. I cleaned up the mess. I never cried. I didn't need to. I sang to find the Prince of Peace, and He rescued me from the evil clutches of the buttered-floor chicken. He saved me from the stink.

The Savior lives, and He has a to-do list just like we do, but His to-do list is to help us get ours done. Happily. No, not just happily but joyfully. And the angels in the midnight church choir sang me the Savior's top priorities on His to-do list:

> He lives to silence all my fears.
> He lives to wipe away my tears.
> He lives to calm my troubled heart.
> He lives all blessings to impart.[83]

The Savior lives and wants us to look to Him and be happy. He will help us accomplish all we need to if we keep a heart full of song. Singing leaves no room to remember that you are *always* picking up knightly socks or that no one *ever* appreciates your cooking or that you *just* bought those dang tires. As we work to build the kingdom and seek the Prince of Peace through song, He will help His princess sisters sing away the mishaps, the trials, the frustrations, and the ugliness—and we will be left with that royal feeling we crave.

Angry Afterthoughts

I think at the end of our mortal life when we finally cross through the veil and look back at our time here on earth, we will be surprised to learn how many thoughts weren't our own. The Holy Ghost whispers the good, and the adversary whispers the bad—and we get to choose, receiving wages from whomever we obey.[84]

I love to be inside the temple, where the Spirit is unrestrained and I am just me. Inside that quiet place, I surprise myself because my little princess head is often empty, free from the usual self-deprecating thoughts, free from the normal harsh judgments. I am normally not hard on myself when I'm in the temple. For the most part, I am just empty-headed and loving it! I listen to others and feel peaceful.

One day in the Salt Lake Temple, a worker was telling me a beautiful story about her sweet daughter's patriarchal blessing and how it mentioned

---

83 Medley, Samuel, "I Know That My Redeemer Lives," *Hymns*, no. 136.
84 See D&C 29:45.

that Heavenly Father loved her and kept her by His side. I smiled to myself as I thought of what a special girl the temple worker's daughter had to be. I smiled all the way out of the locker room and down the hallway to the elevator as I headed for the exit.

Once outside the temple, I began to wonder why Heavenly Father chose that temple worker's daughter to keep by His side. I wondered why He hadn't chosen me.

As I got into the elevator to go down into the parking garage, I thought about my own patriarchal blessing. *Mine* didn't say anything like that. As I got out of the elevator at the bottom floor, my thoughts were almost as dark as the parking garage. Jealousy crept into my heart as I considered what the temple worker had told me.

Why wasn't I *by Heavenly Father's side?* I wondered. *Why didn't* my *blessing say that?* I got into my car and threw my purse on the passenger seat. I was hurt. *Wasn't* I *important enough to be by Heavenly Father's side?* By the time I was pulling out of the parking stall, I was mad.

Driving through the garage, I became more and more angry. As I recklessly navigated my car through the narrow turns, I realized I was being ridiculous. Why shouldn't one of my princess sisters get attention from Heavenly Father? I recognized that I did not initially react this way; it wasn't until I was outside the protected walls of the temple and nearing my car that I had started to get angry.

So I sang. I didn't just turn on the radio to be at the whim of whatever phony joy came through the speakers, but I sang a song that pointed my mouth, my breath, and my heart toward my Savior.

At first, I didn't feel like singing, but I sang anyway, and slowly I started to feel like singing. I entered the on-ramp that led me out of the darkness of the garage and into the sunlight, which splashed into my car and warmed my face. I had not been singing long, just a verse, but I had totally and completely sung away the yucky, jealous, bitter, stinky feelings inside me. All I had left was a soul-smiling, sweet-smelling gladness. I was bursting with joy for a girl I didn't know who was held close to our King.

Our first reactions to love and share are natural. That's us. That's the princess in us. Satan needs time (and not a *lot* of it) to put thoughts of things unfair and things unjust into our heads. When we allow these angry afterthoughts, we become embittered, jealous, unforgiving, unloving, and un-princess-like. When we entertain these thoughts, we stink.

A prime example of this happened with my friend Brandy. She told me how her sister had committed to babysit her son but had later recanted the offer. The princess inside Brandy understood and showed love, telling her sister she would surely work something out; however, in the twenty minutes it took her to drive from her sister's house to mine, Satan whispered his angry afterthoughts into Brandy's heart, reminding her of all the times *she* had babysat for her sister. These reawakened memories of past promises broken and the many times she had rescued her sister, her sisters, and her whole entire family! No one in her family would help her! They *never* helped her! Ever! They *never* had! They *never* would!

By the time Brandy arrived at my house, she was livid. She told me the whole story, beginning with her immediate princess understanding of her sister's circumstances and the love they had parted with and ending with the twenty minutes of angry afterthoughts that finally led to a frazzled end and a crying baby.

Afterthoughts are the bad guys of our hearts, and we have a fierce opponent when we let them fester. I wondered how the story would have ended had Brandy sung when she first felt those angry afterthoughts coming on. Or better yet, what if she had already been singing as she left her sister's house—before any angry afterthoughts could even have been planted?

If we sing, Satan can't plant seeds of destruction in our hearts, which is important because those seeds grow fast. Angry afterthoughts are the cause of contention and the fire of unforgiveness. If Satan doesn't distract you with "almost" good songs on the radio or "almost" good media on the television or the Internet and you allow your mind to sit empty, he will fill it.

When I am not silently pondering and keeping a prayer in my heart or a Savior-seeking song in my head, Satan often fills it with self-deprecating thoughts and family frustrations, both of which can be avoided if we keep a song in our hearts.

Another seed Satan plants in my empty head sprouts terrible arguments with other people . . . who *aren't* there. And better yet, the arguments are over things that never happened.

I will sometimes be arguing with someone in my head for a lengthy several minutes before I snap out of it and realize that, not only is this person not even *with* me, but we're fighting over something that never even *happened*!

And even worse—I am now in a bad mood!

Apparently, I am not alone in my anger-building, fictitious arguments. It is common! I took a poll during three consecutive speeches I gave to Relief Society sisters. In all three groups, I asked if they had ever argued in their head with someone who wasn't there over something that had never happened. In all three speeches, almost every sister raised her hand.

I told my husband, and he couldn't believe it. I guess it's a sisters thing.

What are we allowing inside of us? It's not like we don't have anything better to do, right?

We, as sisters in Zion, are fighting with people who aren't there over things that never happened. The people aren't there! The things we're fighting about *never* even happened! I don't know if I can say this enough to let it sink in. These arguments leave us grumpy. They bring us down, and they keep us from hearing and feeling the Holy Spirit. Seriously, Satan must *love* doing this to us.

One evening, I was leaning over my sink doing dishes with a blank mind (Danger! Danger!). I had no spiritual question I was pondering, no lesson I was planning, no better-wife ideas I was trying to come up with. I was just "zoning" as I washed my dishes.

In my blank mind, which is Satan's favorite potting soil, I began to think about my next grocery trip. I needed some eggs because I planned to make some cookies later that week. In my mind, I went to the store and got the eggs and some other groceries and waited in a long line for the checker. The checker was moving slowly.

So slowly.

Behind me, someone rudely shouted for the checker to call another cashier to the front. I saw the cashier rapidly scanning someone else's groceries. She looked so frazzled. My eyebrows furrowed, and I turned around and told the lady behind me to chill.

The lady didn't like my comment and took her basket, which was overflowing with groceries, and pushed it hard so it hit the back of my wheelchair. I dropped the eggs, and they broke. I turned around, and we got into a terrible verbal argument over how impatient she was and how rude I am and how . . . wait a minute. I wasn't at the store. I was at home. I was washing dishes. I didn't even *know* that lady!

I was flustered, as if my fantasy had been reality and I had really argued with a stranger in the middle of the grocery store. I felt drained. And weird.

I didn't feel happy. I didn't feel like laughing. So I sang.

I sang my fallback song, "I Love to See the Temple."

> I love to see the temple.
> I'm going there someday.
> To feel the Holy Spirit,
> To listen and to pray.[85]

85 Perry, Janice Kapp, "I Love to See the Temple," *Children's Songbook*, 95.

Singing this song brought the Prince of Peace. I was left with the same calm feeling I get when I am in the temple. Heavenly Father has said that our bodies are a temple,[86] and when we sing, they can feel that way.

I have found that when I begin to think self-deprecating thoughts, become frustrated with my family, or have make-believe arguments, I just need to sing out loud. The Prince of Peace lets my soul feel as if I am one of the angels who sings by God's throne—and my soul doesn't long to be there with God because He comes to me.

President Hinckley told a story of a young mother who, like us, missed her King. He shares:

> Some years ago in the Salt Lake Tabernacle, Elder Marion D. Hanks conducted a panel discussion. Included in that panel was an attractive and able young woman, divorced, the mother of seven children then ranging in ages from 7 to 16. She said that one evening she went across the street to deliver something to a neighbor. Listen to her words, as I recall them:
>
>> As I turned around to walk back home, I could see my house lighted up. I could hear echoes of my children as I had walked out of the door a few minutes earlier. They were saying: "Mom, what are we going to have for dinner?" "Can you take me to the library?" "I have to get some poster paper tonight." Tired and weary, I looked at that house and saw the light on in each of the rooms. I thought of all of those children who were home waiting for me to come and meet their needs. My burdens felt heavier than I could bear.
>>
>> I remember looking through tears toward the sky, and I said, "Dear Father, I just can't do it tonight. I'm too tired. I can't face it. I can't go home and take care of all those children alone. Could I just come to You and stay with You for just one night? I'll come back in the morning."
>>
>> I didn't really hear the words of reply, but I heard them in my mind. The answer was: "No, little

one, you can't come to me now. You would never
wish to come back. But I can come to you."[87]

Heavenly Father will come to us when we invite Him near through song.
He will take away anything that chastises our peace. As we busily build
the kingdom of God, let's invite Him for a visit. If we sing, He will help
us accomplish our to-do lists and keep our laugh ready. And when we sing
away whatever stinks, we are left pure—like the temple.

Singing allows room for only the Holy Spirit to comfort us, guide us,
and teach us truths. As we sing, Heavenly Father will lengthen our stride as
we *do our duty with a heart full of song*—whatever that duty is.

I can stay seated for the rest of my mortal life because I know that as
I *put my shoulder to the wheel* and *do my duty with a heart full of song*, the
Savior will take the stink of sadness, sorrow, hurt, fear, and frustration
away. Savior-seeking songs remind me of how temporary this earthly life is
and how someday I will live again with Heavenly Father. And on that day,
I will stand.

Until then, I will sing so I can have peace, so I can feel the presence of
the Prince of Peace. I will sing so I can be worthy to have Him rescue me.

Keeping a song—a prayer—always in our hearts will keep our minds
as clean as they are when inside the holy temple. "When we do this," Sister
Elaine S. Dalton says, "we can confidently enter the holy temples of God
with a knowledge that we are worthy to go where the Lord Himself goes.
When we are worthy, we can not only *enter* the temple, the temple can
enter us."[88]

As we keep a prayer in our hearts and sing, we keep our temples—
our bodies—pure before the Lord. And just like a temple dedication, we
rededicate ourselves to the Lord when we sing away the stink and sing to
prevent it. As we sing, we blow a kiss to our Heavenly Father, and He gives
us His promised blessing upon our heads—a crown, to remind us who
and Whose we are.

---

87 Hinckley, Gordon B., "In the Arms of His Love," *Ensign*, Nov. 2006.
88 Dalton, Elaine S., "Look toward Eternity!" *Ensign*, Nov. 2006.

Chapter 5
SMILE

Let your light shine.

As we blow a kiss to our Heavenly Father each day, He will remind us of our royal heritage, and we will feel closer to Him. When we are kind to others, He will show us kindness. When we don eternal eyes, we will see others' unique purposes and their individual worth. When we seek the Savior through songs, we will find Him.

All of these acts—being kind, seeing individual worth, and singing—are enough to remind us of who we are and will keep us focused on building our straight and narrow path that leads to our happily ever after. But there is one last important step that no princess can dismiss as we remember our royal heritage and blow Heavenly Father a kiss. Sister Elaine S. Dalton, former General Young Women president, shared how we can be examples to others and beautiful examples of princesses on earth when she counseled us to "smile every day."[89]

Smile

As we blow a kiss to our Heavenly Father and take the time each day to be kind to someone, we can't help but smile, especially if the kindness was difficult to offer. When another driver cuts me off on the freeway, I grit my teeth, furrow my eyebrows, and tell them how much I love them and how much I care that they are in a hurry. I apologize for being in their way, and I change lanes. Of course, the other driver is long gone by then, but as I show them kindness—kindness they don't even see—I have to smile at myself because of my efforts. It just feels good to be kind. And I feel that royal feeling when I am.

---

89 Dalton, Elaine S., "An Example of the Believers," *New Era*, Jan. 2009.

The same result occurs when we see ourselves and others as we are—Heavenly Father's spirit sons and daughters who are worth everything He hath, er, has. When I wait in a long line at the store, surrounded by my brothers and sisters, I can't help but smile as I pray in my heart to see them as Heavenly Father does. The wrinkles on their faces or the tattoos on their arms tell a much bigger story when I have eternal eyes. My heart swells with love for them—all of them—and I want to give them all bear-hugs . . . though I refrain and settle for giving them smiles instead.

Likewise, singing Savior-seeking songs makes me smile! I once worked a long day, teaching several seminary classes. One teacher was sick, so I taught his class as well and had no break. In each class, we sang Savior-seeking songs, and when I came home, I listened to more music on the Church's youth website while I did laundry and made dinner.

When my husband came home an hour later, I beamed at him. "I've been smiling all day! I don't know why."

He couldn't hear me, so I turned the music off and said it again, only the second time, I knew why I had been smiling all day: my day had been filled with Savior-seeking music!

Smiling, our final step in blowing a kiss to our Heavenly Father, is a given! If we do the first three steps, we won't be able to hold the fourth one in. We will smile because we feel like smiling.

Maybe I should add a disclaimer to the last paragraph. Being kind, seeing others' individual worth, and singing are extremely effective at causing smiles, but sometimes, just sometimes, they aren't enough. Sometimes this beautiful mortal life tries to steal our smiles. Sometimes in life, no matter how kind we are or how much we sing, bad things happen. Sometimes we experience severe trials, and despite our efforts to build the kingdom, we just plain don't feel like princesses, and we really don't feel like smiling.

I mean, what princess feels like smiling when her prince has never come? Other princesses she grew up with have their own little princes and princesses. Her prince must have been eaten by the dragon. What princess feels like smiling when she so often must leave her castle to spend her days in the doctor's office? What princess feels like smiling when she works two jobs just to feed her family?

Our personal princess storybooks are rarely written like the fairy-tale movie scripts. It's *easy* to watch the movie princesses smile through their trials. From the moment they wake up in their once upon a time to the moment they lie down in their happily ever after, they're smiling.

Of course. It's easy for them. Their fairy tale is assured, their ending written. It lasts ninety minutes. Anyone can do anything for ninety minutes.

We, however, are in between hardbound covers, lost within our own stories' pages, not knowing how our chapters will end or what the next ones are even called. We seem to be writing page after page of adversity with the nub of a tiny pencil we found under a stale french fry between the seats of our almost-broken-down car. But President Dieter F. Uchtdorf told us that our trials don't hold that nubby pencil; we do. He said, "It is [our] reaction to adversity, not the adversity itself, that determines how [our] life's story will develop."[90]

Even though our stories include several chapters of adversity, we can react well. We can react royally. We can smile in the face of the storms that try to soak our hope and dampen our spirits. President Thomas S. Monson shared the message from the poet Ella Wheeler Wilcox:

> It is easy enough to be pleasant,
> When life flows by like a song,
> But the man worth while is one who will smile,
> When everything goes dead wrong.
> For the test of the heart is trouble,
> And it always comes with the years,
> And the smile that is worth the praises of earth
> Is the smile that shines through tears.[91]

This beautiful poem describes how a beautiful princess will wear a beautiful smile while she's in the midst of a not-so-beautiful trial. This poem describes a princess who, regardless of neighborhood, clothing brands, or education, smiles. She smiles when she's tired. She smiles when she's grumpy. She smiles when she just plain doesn't feel like smiling. A beautiful princess is one who builds the kingdom with her bare hands while she blows a kiss to her Father in Heaven and smiles every day—no matter how she feels.

What?

I can hear it now: *We should be honest with our emotions! It's better to let our anger out! No one should smile if they don't mean it!*

I have seen these ideas on Facebook, Twitter, and texts and have heard them in casual conversations with friends.

90 Uchtdorf, Dieter F., "Your Happily Ever After," *Ensign*, May 2010, 126.
91 "Worth While," in *The Best Loved Poems of the American People*, sel. Hazel Felleman (Garden City, New York: Doubleday, 1936), 144; in Monson, Thomas S., "Meeting Life's Challenges," *Ensign*, Nov. 1993.

Many believe that others should understand that they look grumpy because they *feel* grumpy. They think others should understand that they look sad because they *are* sad. They think others should understand that they look tired because they *are* tired.

But the thing is, when you let your emotions show like that, other people do understand, but frankly, most don't care. They have their own grumps and their own sadnesses. And they're tired too. They are focused on themselves, just like everyone else.

I mean, after all, we've got to take care of number one. How can we smile and cheer up another when we're the one who needs cheering? How can our smile brighten someone's day when we feel so gloomy? Our needs must be met, and who will meet them if not us?

This emotional rationalization gives us excuses to frown and be stressed and vent when we feel like it. When we believe others should make way for our grumpiness, we allow ourselves to stay unhappy and often bring others down with us. President Dieter F. Uchtdorf shares how princesses can find balance and blessings when they refuse to be driven by their own emotions: "While there are times when it is prudent to look first to our own needs, in the long run it doesn't lead to lasting happiness."[92]

Lasting happiness, the kind that endures through personal struggles, comes when we put others' feelings and needs before our own. Lasting happiness comes when we smile at others in spite of how we feel. Lasting happiness comes to princesses who act like princesses.

I'm certain Snow White didn't feel like smiling. I mean, she'd just run away from everything and everyone she knew and loved, and she had *barely* escaped being a homicide victim. She had every reason to mope around the dwarves' cottage. Certainly, at the very least, those dwarves should have been making *her* a pie.

And it doesn't make sense that Cinderella, parentless and hopeless, could smile as she made up the satin sheets of her evil stepsisters' beds—I mean, come on; who can smile and do chores at the same time, let alone smile as you're doing your *sisters'* chores?

And even before she knew she was a princess, Aurora, living in the woods with three fuddy old ladies, smiled as she danced through the forest with her animal friends.

Like Cinderella, Snow White, and Aurora, we do not smile because everything (or anything) is going our way; instead, we smile because we're

92   Uchtdorf, Dieter F., "Happiness, Your Heritage," *Ensign*, Nov. 2008.

princesses and that's what princesses do. As we smile and *look* like princesses, we begin to *feel* like princesses.

Only a princess can smile in the face of fatigue or sorrow or sadness or stress. The saying goes, "Sometimes your joy is the source of your smile, but sometimes your smile can be the source of your joy."[93] As we heed President Uchtdorf's counsel to look past our own needs and force our princess faces to smile at others despite how we feel, we will find that smiling when we don't feel like smiling actually makes us feel like smiling!

Researchers in Echnische Universität in Munich Germany took a functional MRI to measure brain activity and smiling. The research found that smiling activates our brain's emotion and happiness wiring.[94] These researchers found that we actually make ourselves happy when we "fake" a smile! We can make ourselves feel happy enough to smile just by smiling. To make ourselves feel happy, we smile first and feel happy second.

As a teenager, I was in a play called *South Pacific*. It was through a local community theater, and I played a nurse in the chorus. During one performance, another nurse and I thought it would be funny to "fake" smile throughout the entire show. Each time we went out to sing or dance, we grinned as wide as we possibly could, showing all of our teeth in sloppy, fake smiles. However, we could maintain each fake smile only for a few seconds before we erupted into giggles and real smiles. We found that our fake smiles not only put real smiles on our faces but also pulled real smiles out of others.

Do you remember a time when someone smiled at you? Do you remember how you smiled back? Or maybe you were caught off guard (that happens), and you smiled after they left. Remember how good you felt? I bet you smiled at someone right afterward. "Two studies from 2002 and 2011 at Uppsala University in Sweden confirmed that other people's smiles actually suppress the control we usually have over our facial muscles,

---

93 "*Thich Nhat Hanh Quotes,*" *Quotes.net,* STANDS4 LLC, 2012, Retrieved 6 Nov. 2012, <http://www.quotes.net/quote/13944>.

94 Hennenlotter, Andreas, Christian Dresel, Florian Castrop, Andres O. Ceballos-Baumann, Afra M. Wohlschläger, and Bernhard Haslinger. "The link between facial feedback and neural activity within central circuitries of emotion— New insights from Botulinum toxin–induced denervation of frown muscles." *Cerebral Cortex* 19, no. 3 (2009): 537-542, Retrieved 04 May 2013, http://cercor.oxfordjournals.org/content/19/3/537.short; Savitz, Eric, "The Untapped Power of Smiling," *Forbes.com,* Retrieved 04 May 2013, http://www.forbes.com/sites/ericsavitz/2011/03/22/the-untapped-power-of-smiling/.

compelling us to smile. They also showed that it's very difficult to frown when looking at someone who is smiling."[95] Smiling is a chain reaction.

I put this idea to the test once and smiled at everyone I met. Most smiled back. However, some didn't. At first, I thought this study must be bogus; it wasn't working, and I was smiling as big as I could. My smile was supposed to suppress the control others had over their face and make them smile too, and it wasn't doing that.

But then I started to really look at the people who didn't return the smile. I noticed that even though their face didn't smile, they twitched. Some would twitch into an almost fake smile, making their lips disappear as they stretched their mouths wide from ear to ear. Some mouths would twitch into an almost fake smile as they squished their bottom lips into their top lips, making their chins wrinkle up. And one lady I passed twitched her mouth into an upside-down smile. I guess it was the very best she could do.

Even when fake smiles or upside-down smiles are not returned to us, we know our efforts to lift others are effective. Seeing a smile makes a person smile (or do the best they can at it), and smiling activates their brains' circuitry of happiness. Who knew that smiling at others could be such a technological service project and that tinkering with someone's brain could activate their happiness? And while we're activating their happiness, our own smiles are causing our happiness circuits to explode!

Happiness is only part of the consequences of smiling. Penn State University researchers found that "when we smile we not only appear more likeable and courteous, but we're actually perceived to be more competent."[96] This likely doesn't surprise you. I'm certain you already know the effects of smiling. If we go to the bank where two tellers are open, one of whom has tired eyes and a smile and one of whom has tired eyes and is expressionless, of course we will choose the smiler.

My husband, Whit, and I were stopped at a traffic light on the way home one afternoon. I was driving, and Whit was telling me a story. He talks with his hands, and he was very into the story as he spoke animatedly.

A tan sedan pulled up next to us on my husband's side, and I looked over. The driver and I and made eye contact, and I smiled. He smiled too. Of course he did—smiles suppress other people's facial control. But his smile was huge. And he didn't stop smiling. He smiled big and kept looking

95   Savitz, Eric, "The Untapped Power of Smiling," *Forbes.com*, Retrieved 04 May 2013, http://www.forbes.com/sites/ericsavitz/2011/03/22/the-untapped-power-of-smiling/.

96   Ibid.

into our car, seeming to try to get my attention again. I actively avoided him, squished myself back into the seat, and hid behind my unaware husband, who continued talking with his hands and telling his story.

The traffic light turned green, and I sped through. Our turn was coming up, so I got into the median and waited for an opening. As I turned left, I watched the tan sedan quickly flip a U-turn and come back. He followed us down the road.

I couldn't keep my husband out of the loop any longer. Cautiously looking into my rearview mirror, I said, "Um, Whit? There's no need to be alarmed, but there's a man in a tan sedan following us."

Whit told me not to go home, and we pulled over in front of a church. (Nothing bad ever happens in front of a church, right?) The tan sedan pulled up next to us, and we rolled down our windows.

He yelled into our car, not at me but at my husband, "Hey, dude, is this your girlfriend?"

My husband and I looked at each other, and he replied, "Um, no, she's my wife."

There was a short pause, and the tan-sedan man said, "Well, she is a beautiful lady." And he drove away.

I am sure this guy passed a lot of beautiful girls that day. We were right by a college campus, and it was lunchtime. There were cute girls everywhere. But he followed me—well, he followed my smile—which leaves only one conclusion: beauty isn't found in a gorgeous body or even in a face. It's found in teeth.

On another day as I drove on the freeway, I made eye contact with a passing motorcyclist. Well, at least I think I made eye contact with him. He had a big helmet on with a reflective visor covering his eyes, but he looked my way.

I smiled. I don't know what he did because the visor blocked his face, but he sped up to pass me.

My exit came a few seconds later, and I took it. But as I was rounding the bend of the road, I watched this motorcyclist slow down, cut quickly through four lanes of traffic, and follow me off. I wanted to think he had almost missed his exit, but it seemed suspicious.

At the light, I turned right. And so did he.

Then I took a quick left. He did too.

A traffic light in front of me turned yellow then red, but this motorcyclist was creeping me out, so I ran it . . . and so did he.

I wanted to run the next traffic light, but there were already several cars piled up, waiting for it to change. It was a one-way street, and I was in the far left lane next to a sidewalk. As the light remained forever red, I held as still as possible and darted my eyes between the side mirrors and the rearview mirror to keep an eye on the creepy motorcyclist. But he didn't stay behind me. In my side mirror, I watched him manhandle his motorcycle onto the sidewalk and walk it toward me. I looked straight ahead and pretended not to notice.

I wasn't scared—I mean, it was broad daylight, and there were cars and people everywhere. I just didn't know what was going on.

As he pulled up next to me, I looked over and smiled. What else could I do? He motioned for me to roll down my window. I did. Barely.

The motorcyclist leaned toward the car and flipped up his visor. His face squished out of the helmet as he smiled, tilted his head, and, very suave-like, asked, "Hi. Are you married?"

I went home, told my husband, then said, "Yeah, I've still got it."

Getting hit on has got to be one of the best compliments. It means someone thinks we're beautiful, but it also, and more importantly, means someone thinks we're friendly enough to approach. The highest compliment someone can give us is wanting to be with us. Smiling has a way of breaking down the barriers and making others feel comfortable. Everyone—men and women—wants to be around the person who makes them feel the best. Everyone wants to be around the people who smile.

Jenny is a friend of mine with a beautiful and well-used smile. She went on a trip to New York City, which has been dubbed the city with "the most neurotic and unfriendly people in America . . . according to a Cambridge University 'personality map.'" [97] As Jenny walked the sidewalks from her hotel to an off-Broadway theater four blocks away, she beamed at potentially neurotic and unfriendly passersby. Despite the fact that the city streets where she walked were trampled by the country's self-proclaimed most stressed individuals, Jenny got asked out on a date by four different people.

Smiling is the magic people-magnet. Smiling brings friends and success and lasting happiness! A smiler seems—and *is*—happier. In a thirty-year study by the University of California Berkley, researchers "examined the smiles of students in an old yearbook, and measured their well-being and

97 "New Yorkers are neurotic and unfriendly, says Cambridge University 'personality map,'" Retrieved 04 May 2013, http://www.telegraph.co.uk/news/worldnews/northamerica/usa/2779683/New-Yorkers-are-neurotic-and-unfriendly-says-Cambridge-University-personality-map.html.

success throughout their lives. By measuring the smiles in the photographs the researchers were able to predict: how fulfilling and long lasting their marriages would be, how highly they would score on standardized tests of well-being and general happiness, and how inspiring they would be to others. The widest smilers consistently ranked highest in all of the above."[98]

Smiling is a science! Successful author and entrepreneur Dan Miller advised all to "smile big. Try to feel defeated or discouraged and smile big at the same time. You can't. A big smile gives you confidence." [99] A big smile gives us confidence and competence and makes us appear more likeable and beautiful—all the qualities of a perfect princess. The effects of our smiles are great, but the source of our smiles is even greater.

After I was paralyzed, my confidence was severely attacked. I earned it back little by little as I worked hard to become more independent and do things I once did. People often ask me what the hardest thing was that I ever had to relearn, and I have no answer for them. With my newly paralyzed body, everything was hard. There was no difficulty difference between relearning to drive a car and relearning how to hold a fork. But with a lot of effort, I relearned how to do things by myself one task at a time.

The very first thing I learned how to do was put on my make-up. To put that in perspective, the second thing I learned how to do was eat. (Hey, we princesses have our priorities!) But the best thing I ever learned how to do by myself was pick my nose . . . . You know, you don't ever appreciate picking your own nose until you've had to ask someone to do it for you.

It was during this time of relearning that I met a man who had come over to look at my car. I was selling my sedan for another kind of car that would fit my wheelchair and me better. We were by the car, and I was trying to tell him all the exciting things about it—power windows, CD player, seat belts—but he didn't seem interested in any of that. He just asked me why I was in a wheelchair.

I told him briefly how I had become wheelchair bound and then upped the excitement and told him about the roomy trunk and excellent windshield wipers.

He didn't care and asked me how long I'd been paralyzed.

I told him a few months and redirected his attention to the brand-spanking-new tires.

98 Savitz, Eric, "The Untapped Power of Smiling," *Forbes.com*, Retrieved 04 May 2013, http://www.forbes.com/sites/ericsavitz/2011/03/22/the-untapped-power-of-smiling/.

99 Miller, Dan, "I need more self-confidence," *48Days.com*, Retrieved 04 May 2013, http://www.48days.com/2011/06/20/i-need-more-self-confidence/.

He wasn't interested and asked me about my hands.

I was relatively irritated because I really wanted to sell my car and wanted him to buy it. I told him they were paralyzed and I couldn't move them and then told him about the exciting cup holders—not just in the front seat but in the back.

He didn't care and asked me about my legs—could I feel them at all?

I told him no and then half laughed, half screamed inside my head, *Just buy my car, already!*

I started to tell him about the great air conditioner when he stopped me midsentence, folded his arms across his chest, looked down at me and asked, "Meg, how can you still smile?"

I stared up at him—annoyed that he obviously wasn't going to buy my car and doubly annoyed that he would have the gall to ask me this question. The question itself wasn't annoying, but the unspoken part of that question was, *How can you still smile when clearly your life can hold no joy?*

I was mad! *How can he even stand there like that and wonder? Doesn't he know about my awesome family and their awesome support?* I thought. *And doesn't he know what I have learned to do? Doesn't he know how hard I've worked? Doesn't he know I can pick my nose? Doesn't he know I can tie my shoes? Doesn't he know I can brush my teeth? Doesn't he know how liberating it feels to make your own Jell-O or brush your own hair? Can't he see how hard I've worked and just why I have cause to smile?*

The passion inside me was fiery. I opened my mouth to tell him all these reasons and explain just why *I* had cause to smile, but none of that came out. I couldn't say any of it. The Spirit took hold of my heart, and the passion inside me exploded as I told him the only true answer there was: "I have a testimony of Jesus Christ."

He looked down at me with a blank expression, seeming to expect a follow-up explanation.

And I looked up at him, unable to give him one.

I couldn't take it back. And I didn't want to take it back because, of all the things I have that make me smile, and of all thing things I can do that make me smile, the only reason I *can* smile each and every day is that I have a testimony of Jesus Christ. I have a testimony that He created the earth. I have a testimony that He came to it. I have a testimony that He atoned and died. And above all, I have a testimony that He lives.

He is my Brother, my Savior, and if I obey His commandments, He is my Friend. His Atonement paid the price for me to enter into eternal life so I can live forever with Him. When I keep my Savior in my heart, I am buoyed up with my testimony of Him and the plan of happiness He made possible, the plan of happiness that makes us just that: happy. It is depicted as only circles on a chalkboard or clipart on a screen but is true and real and eternal nonetheless.

I lived in the premortal existence, and my Heavenly Father wrapped His arms around me before He sent me here to earth, and if I live righteously now, I will see Him again in that top final circle of the celestial kingdom, where I'll live with Him—and like Him—forever.

And they don't make wheelchairs in forever.

The plan of happiness is real. I know it is. During one of our weekly family home evenings, my husband and I read an article from the *Ensign* about it. We often read *Ensign* articles together, but this time was different.

As Whit read about the resurrection, a powerful feeling came over me, and I knew what he was reading was true. At once, I saw someone standing in our living room on the rug.

I knew the veil shielded this person from my mortal eyes, but my spiritual eyes knew he was there. I knew where his feet were as he stood on our living room rug. I knew how tall he was. I knew how wide he was. And most importantly, I knew why he had come.

His message enveloped me with a force uninhibited. I was unable to stop the tears. I did not want to move. I looked to where he stood, unable to see him but unable to look away. And though my mortal ears never heard a word, my heart heard the message loud and clear: The resurrection is real. That is all this person came to tell me. Knowing that the resurrection is real and the plan of happiness is true makes me feel, well, happy. Let me share a story found in my book *When Life Gets Hard . . .* :

> I remember going with my husband to one of his performances at a Hispanic culture fair. At the time, he was my boyfriend, and he played the guitar in a Brazilian style called Bossa Nova. At the event, I sat at our table and enjoyed all the musicians playing their different styles of music from all of the Hispanic countries. After my husband's group performed, he joined me at our table, where we ate beans and rice as we continued to listen to the bands play. I was surprised when the music changed from live, acoustic music to a recorded heavy rhythmic beat. I looked to the stage to see two Latin dancers start dancing.

My heart started to sink as I felt the vibrations of the music through my wheelchair. This was the very first time I had seen Latin dancers or even heard Latin dancing music since I had been paralyzed. My eyes unexpectedly welled up with tears, and I didn't dare blink, or the tears would fall, and everyone would know I was crying. I didn't want anyone to feel sad for me, but I knew the tears would eventually fall, so I excused myself from the table and went into the hallway. I rolled behind a large plant and hid. And then I cried.

As I cried, I prayed. I told Heavenly Father I was sorry I was so weak. I tried to be strong, but I didn't always know how. I told Him I knew this earthly life was temporary and I knew I would walk and dance again. I asked Heavenly Father to increase my faith in the plan of salvation.

I stopped crying immediately. My heavy heart lightened, and I could feel the Savior's presence testifying that the plan of salvation was true. I lived in heaven before I came to earth. I will be resurrected. I will stand. And I will dance.

With the knowledge that I can have eternal life with my Heavenly Father in a not-so-distant happily ever after, I can enjoy this life, walking or not. With the knowledge that my Savior died so I can live again, I can enjoy this life, standing or not. And with the knowledge that my Savior lives, I can enjoy this life, dancing or not. "Men are, that they might have joy,"[100] and because I know all of this, I have joy.

Because we know these truths, our spiritual eyes have been opened, and we become spiritually minded. Blowing a kiss and being kind, seeing worth, and singing will keep us spiritually minded throughout the day, and it gives us opportunities to serve and seek the Savior. As we stay spiritually minded and rely on the Savior, we will know the truth Nephi spoke of when he said that to be "spiritually-minded is life eternal."[101]

Spiritually Minded Is Life Eternal.

Spiritually **M**inded **I**s **L**ife **E**ternal.

S.M.I.L.E.

As we blow a kiss and stay spiritually minded, we cannot help but smile. I attended a Christ-centered Easter assembly at a seminary, where we learned about His life and Resurrection for ninety minutes. I watched the program twice. Then I had to leave to run errands.

---

100   2 Nephi 2:25.
101   2 Nephi 9:39.

My list wasn't any different from previous days, but *something* was different—I couldn't stop smiling. I smiled at the grocery store, in the car, at the post office, and by myself as I put groceries away in my kitchen. Just focusing on my Savior, who opened the way into everlasting life, made me smile.

And smiling gives me confidence. And competence. And likeability. And above all, that royal feeling.

Our Peculiar Duty

With the Savior as the source of our smile and so many wonderful consequences of smiling, it surprises me how few people do it.

My husband and I recently attended a fancy black-tie event in Salt Lake City with hundreds of the most well-dressed and outwardly beautiful people in attendance. Among the guests were models, reporters, photographers, and news media.

We saw men in tailored suits paired with alligator-skin shoes and cufflinks on crisp-collared shirts. The women had perfect hair and perfect make-up and perfectly expensive dresses. Their glittering ball gowns looked like they cost more than my car. These women were walk-off-the-magazine beautiful. And as I looked around the room at these beautiful and elegant women, I noticed that, unless there was a news camera right up on one of them, not one of them was smiling.

My heart was sad, and I thought to myself, *These are beautiful people. But I wonder how much more beautiful they would be if they would only smile.*

The words from the musical *Annie* came to my mind, the ones that talk about not being fully dressed, even in your best clothes, if you don't have a smile. [102]

I wondered why these women took the time to find a beautiful dress and do their hair and their make-up so beautifully if they were only going to repel everyone who looked their way with their cold, nonsmiling faces. I wondered if these women thought disinterested stares and pursed lips were pretty.

They aren't.

President Packer shares an experience about being assigned to stake conferences in Western Samoa. Because of rain, the plane that was supposed to come get President Packer, the mission president, and others couldn't land, so they decided to take a boat to the island they were going to. None of them knew a terrible tropical storm had hit and they were heading straight into it.

102   See Charning, Martin; Thomas Meehan; and Charles Strouse, *Annie,* 1977.

As they approached the other island, they searched for the light on the hill and the lower light directly under it that would help lead them through the narrow passage in the dangerous reef. But through the darkness, the group saw only the top light. The two elders who were waiting for the boat had fallen asleep and neglected to turn on the second, lower light.

The captain of the small boat tried as best he could to get to the shore, but the storm was too fierce, and he couldn't see the way. He tried many futile attempts to find the passage, but it seemed impossible. Eventually, the boat had to sail forty miles through the storm's thick darkness to another harbor.[103]

While most people probably haven't been surrounded by crashing waves as they've held tightly to a rickety, rocking boat, being in frightening situations is all too familiar to all of us.

For those without the light of the gospel, every day, no matter how well navigated, is packed with crashing waves and thick darkness. Some can see the lighthouse where the Savior's light shines, but the lighthouse alone tells them only where the safety of the land is, not how to get there. This is where the upper and lower lights come in.

This is where *we* come in.

We are the lights along the shore. The upper light shines in our eyes, as said in Matthew: "The light of the body is the eye: if therefore thine eye be single, thy whole body shall be full of light."[104] The light we add to our eyes comes from the Savior as He told the Nephites, "Behold I am the light which ye shall hold up—that which ye have seen me do."[105] As we follow Christ's example and work hard to attend church meetings, read our scriptures, do our visiting teaching, and just be righteous, our eyes increase in light, making the upper light in our eyes shine brighter and brighter.

But in addition to the upper light, we have a second, lower light that must be equally bright: our smiles. We need this lower light to stay brightly lit so others know that we know where the safety of the land is—they might miss the glimmer in our eyes, but they'll never miss the brightness of our smile.

The hymn states:

> Brightly beams our Father's mercy
> From his lighthouse evermore,

---

103   Packer, Boyd K., "The Atonement," *Ensign*, Nov. 2012.
104   Matt. 6:22.
105   3 Nephi 18:24

But to us he gives the keeping
Of the lights along the shore.
Let the lower lights be burning;
Send a gleam across the wave.
Some poor fainting, struggling seaman
You may rescue, you may save.[106]

Our duty is to keep both lights burning so we can show others the way to the safety of the land and, more importantly, so they can also build on the rock of our Redeemer and be lights themselves along the shore.

But we are only good at saving struggling seamen and women if we constantly have both our lights burning. Few sailors are wandering the grocery stores assessing the upper light in our eyes. Just like President Packer and his crew needed the bottom light to be lit to navigate through the dangerous sea, those around us need our bottom lights trimmed and brightly smiling to know that we are firmly built on a solid foundation and not bobbing around in the water.

There is a powerful reminder from the Savior when it comes to keeping our lights burning. Jesus stated, "Neither do men light a candle, and put it under a bushel."[107]

Do we?

Do we, as members of The Church of Jesus Christ of Latter-day Saints, light our spiritual candles with diligent obedience to the gospel only to put those candles under a bushel? President James E. Faust said, "We can let the light within us show in many different ways. It may be as simple as a smile."[108]

But our bright candles are only good on candlesticks. Do we light our candles as we read our scriptures but then pull a bushel of frowning over our heads as we navigate the grocery store aisles? Do we light our candles with fervent prayer only to walk through the county library oblivious to others because we're covered in a bushel of concentration? Do we light our candles every Monday night in diligent family home evening efforts only to cover that light under a bushel of pursed lips and stress the rest of the week?

As members of the Church, we know what it takes to receive the Father's light, and He has named us the "light of the world" and commanded us to let our light so shine before men.[109]

---

106 Bliss, Philip Paul, "Brightly Beams Our Father's Mercy," *Hymns*, no. 335.
107 Matt. 5:15.
108 Faust, James E., "Your Light—A Standard to All Nations," *Ensign*, May 2006.
109 Matt. 5:14–16.

We can't let our light inside us hide! We can't work so hard to light our testimony candles just to hide them under a bushel of tight-lipped frowns. We must hold our testimonies high on candlesticks for the entire world to see. One type of candlestick we have just happens to be made of enamel. Our candlesticks are our teeth—our smiles.

We must smile to hold our enamel candlesticks high, to let our light so shine before the grocery store cashier who is moving in slow motion. We can hold our enamel candlesticks high as we smile and wave at the elementary school kids who are waiting for the bus and every single person we pass in morning traffic.

Holding our candlesticks high might be awkward, especially when no one else is smiling back. People might think we're a little weird, but the Savior Himself has named us "a peculiar people"[110]—so let's act like it!

President Spencer W. Kimball, a member of the Quorum of the Twelve Apostles at the time, said, "We are different. We are a peculiar people. We hope we shall always be unusual and peculiar."[111] Let's be peculiar and smile when it makes more sense to cry. Let's be peculiar and smile when it makes more sense to scoff. Let's be peculiar and smile when it makes more sense to roll our eyes. Let's be peculiar and smile when frowning is all we feel like doing. Let's be peculiar and smile when angry eyes are all we want to muster. Let's smile no matter where we are, no matter who we're with, and no matter what we're doing.

It is our peculiar duty to smile and hold our light high. This is the princess way. This is the way of someone who blows a kiss to Heavenly Father daily and does those things that help her grow in the light of the Savior. This is the way of someone who insists on shining that light by holding her enamel candlestick high.

As others see us smile, they will want to know why. It is the simplest way we can bear our testimonies—it is our teeth-imony!

As members of the true Church, with the fulness of the gospel, let's take every opportunity to bear witness to it. President Uchtdorf counseled, "The most effective way to preach the gospel is through example. If we live according to our beliefs, people will notice. If the countenance of Jesus Christ shines in our lives, if we are joyful and at peace with the world, people

---

110   1 Peter 2:9.

111   Kimball, Spencer W., "In the World but Not of It," *Brigham Young University Speeches of the Year*, 14 May 1968, 10; in "Numbers 1–10," *Old Testament Teacher Resource Manual*, 2003, Retrieved 04 May 2013, http://www.lds.org/manual/old-testament-teacher-resource-manual/numbers-1-10?lang=eng.

will want to know why. One of the greatest sermons ever pronounced on missionary work is this simple thought attributed to Saint Francis of Assisi: 'Preach the gospel at all times and if necessary, use words.'"[112]

We have to smile, even and especially when smiling is difficult, because we can't be examples of light if we look like everyone else. Sister Dalton said, "If you desire to make a difference in the world, *you must be different from the world*."[113] Others watch us. Even if we're surrounded by other members of the Church, if we are smilers, people will watch us. Once, when I was seventeen, a young couple approached me after a sacrament meeting, and they were laughing. They were giggling to each other and said that I had been the height of their entertainment through the meeting as they'd watched me, counting the number of times I smiled at nothing. They laughed together, saying that they've never seen anyone smile so much.

I wasn't even smiling at this young couple—they were seated behind me. But still, my smile reached them, making them smile too. The smile itself is contagious, but so are the feelings of goodness, warmth, and light. We can gain a testimony, and we can give a teeth-imony.

Recently, I was driving down a heavily trafficked road and had to stop at *every single* traffic light. I was late, I was frustrated, and I was stressed. I looked over to see a woman smiling as she chatted with someone on a cell phone headset. She wasn't even looking at me, but her smile made me smile, and I smiled all the way to my errand.

When the Savior appeared in the Americas, His "countenance did smile upon"[114] the people, and as we try to be like Him, we must do the same. We don't even have to *know* someone to wave and smile at them. President James E. Faust said, "The commandment given by the Savior was to love others and yourself. . . . Am I secure in my love of others to smile and say hello to a perfect stranger?"[115]

My husband and I drove through the tiny town of Avon, Utah. We passed by the old wooden city sign that read: "Welcome to Avon—Home of 307 Friendly People." My husband and I were curious and wanted to see if the people of this town really were friendlier than others.

Sure enough, the first car we passed waved wildly to us. We got excited—definitely bitten by the contagiously friendly Avon bug! We saw

112 Uchtdorf, Dieter F., "Waiting on the Road to Damascus," *Ensign*, May 2011, 77.
113 Dalton, Elaine S., "Now Is the Time to Arise and Shine!" *Ensign*, May 2012.
114 3 Nephi 19:25.
115 Faust, James E., "The Value of Self-Esteem," (speech, Salt Lake City, 6 May 2007), *Lds.org*, Retreived 04 May 2013, http://www.lds.org/library/display/0,4945,538-1-4136-1,00.html.

a man doing yard work, and we waved and smiled wildly at him. He, however, just stared at us, probably wondering if he knew us. The sun was bright, and his squinty eyes made it look as if he was scowling. My husband and I determined that he was the 308th person in Avon. If we are not smiling, it really, honestly, truly doesn't matter what else we're doing with our faces. A smile is the only expression we have that makes another person feel good. We must be careful to always smile.

I was embarrassed one time when I was driving on the freeway and saw a very strange car. It was an old clunker packed with odds and ends that practically blocked all the windows. There were magazines and old cups and boxes and a rubber chicken (no joke). I wondered if all of it was coming or going or if that's where it all lived. I stared quizzically as I slowly passed the driver and eyed him as intently as I'd eyed the contents of the car.

Then I shook my head. What was I doing? I sped away, thankful he didn't look over at me to see my furrowed eyebrows and pursed lips. It would have made him feel terrible.

The expressions we wear send messages. We must be careful that ours are sending good ones, because a brief smile can make someone's day just as easily as a seemingly expressionless face can ruin one. No one would stick their tongue out at a passing man or woman in the supermarket, but the end result is somewhat the same if we show them any expression that isn't a smile.

Everyone is searching for light and truth. We know where to find it, but many do not. When they see our faces, they recognize the light. Smiling is such a tiny thing; you might wonder how it could be so meaningful or how one momentary, snaggle-toothed grin could ever make a difference. Let me share a post from Dan Miller:

> The Golden Gate Bridge is the world's leading suicide location. Every two weeks, on average, someone ends their life here. At least twelve hundred people have been seen jumping or have been found in the water since the bridge opened in 1937. . . . Dr. Jerome Motto had a patient who jumped in the mid seventies. "I went to this guy's apartment afterward with the assistant medical examiner," he says. "The guy was in his thirties, lived alone, pretty bare apartment. He'd written a note and left it on his bureau. It said, 'I'm going to walk to the bridge. If one person smiles at me on the way, I will not jump.'"

Wow—what a simple gift. How many people did he meet that day?

What if I had been one of them?[116]

No, really, what if I *had* been one of them?

What if you had been one of them?

In heaven, when we see this man, do you think he will understand when we explain that we had just had a long day? Do you think we could justify our cold looks because we didn't want him to hit on us? Do you think he will forgive us for making eye contact and quickly looking away, pretending not to notice him because we were busy? Do you think we could find the words to explain that we were just zoning and didn't even see him?

I can hear it now: "Oh, Meg, you're so dramatic. Hardly anyone commits suicide. And certainly no one would want to kill themselves just because I didn't smile at them."

No. You're right. Maybe no one will wish to die because you didn't smile at them. But how many people, downtrodden and disheartened, do we pass daily? They likely look fine on the outside, but their hearts are sorely damaged. They're hungrily searching for light and hope and love. So instead of asking how few people will want to die because we don't smile, a better question to ask ourselves is, "How many people can we make come alive if we do?"

Our peculiar duty is to hold our enamel candlesticks high and let the light we borrow from the Savior shine. We must smile. We must do as President Hinckley counseled sisters everywhere to do when he said, "Go forward in life with a twinkle in your eye and a smile on your face, but with great and strong purpose in your heart."[117]

We smile because we princesses know that life doesn't often make us want to smile, so we smile first and feel happy second. We smile because we know Jesus Christ lives, the plan of happiness is real, and we want to bear our teeth-imonies every chance we get. We smile because we know our duty as daughters of the King.

---

116 Miller, Dan, "For the want of a smile," *48Days.com*, Retrieved 04 May 2013, http://www.48days.com/2011/11/22/smile/.

117 Hinckley, Gordon B., "Words of the Prophet: Daughters of the Almighty," *New Era*, Nov. 2003, 4.

Chapter 6
CONCLUSION

THE VEIL THAT SEPARATES US from our heavenly home is thick, and even though Heavenly Father is too far away to hug, we feel His love and presence when we blow Him a kiss.

We can feel His kindness when we're kind. With eternal eyes, we can see our and others' individual worth. He will help us accomplish our to-do lists when our hearts are full of Savior-seeking songs. And we feel like His when we accept our peculiar duty to smile. He reminds us where we came from. He reminds us who we are: His daughters. Daughters of the King.

Princesses.

And even though it might feel as if the princess train derailed years ago, it is still very much on track, charging full steam ahead into eternity. Next stop: happily ever after.

But are we on it?

As far as the royal treatment goes, the train isn't quite what we expected. There aren't velvet seats and satin pillows on which to lounge lazily as we glide along. Instead, we find that the war that began in heaven is still being fiercely fought today—even from our bumpy seats on the train: "And there was war in heaven: Michael and his angels fought against the dragon; and the dragon fought and his angels, And prevailed not; neither was their place found any more in heaven. And the great dragon was cast out, that old serpent, called the Devil, and Satan, which deceiveth the whole world: he was cast out into the earth, and his angels were cast out with him."[118]

The dragon that flies alongside our windows, his breath heavy on the glass, reminds us of the bumpy ride and points out the pleather tears in our less-than-lovely seats. His eternal mission is to thwart our happily

---

118 Revelation 12:7–9.

ever after. He often succeeds in spoiling the ending for other princesses. He whispers to them and "helps" them find their princess-status in other fruitless (and crownless) directions.

He boards some of them on plastic trains with stacks and stacks of beauty magazines, fooling them with the ever-perpetuated lie that a princess needs to look like one. Others he crams into the most popular trains, even though there's no seating, and these duped princesses are cushioned by politically correct acceptance. And still, some princesses are boarded into gold-leafed trains, traveling in the lap of luxury in their plush personal cabins. The dragon feeds them falsehoods on a silver spoon, telling them every princess should live like one.

The dragon runs rampant. It doesn't matter which other train he can lure other princesses to just as long as he can get them off track. As princesses with a knowledge of who we are, where we came from, and most importantly, where we're going, we must remain steadfast on our train, willing to fight the dragon's constant attack.

We don't wear fancy dresses or have perfect hair, but we don the armor of God, wielding swords of truth against the happily-ever-after attackers. We will fight until our train stops and we can safely step off board, resting our tired feet on the golden streets of forever. But until then, we fight. And because we keep our Heavenly Father close through the kisses we blow to Him, we fight happily!

> We are all enlisted till the conflict is o'er;
> Happy are we! Happy are we!
> Soldiers in the army, there's a bright crown in store;
> We shall win and wear it by and by.[119]

The bright crown that awaits us is one we will never take off. It is our crown of eternal life. Though our battle may seem like a never-ending story, we know we will be victorious. President Ezra Taft Benson said, "The final outcome is certain—the forces of righteousness will finally win. What remains to be seen is where each of us personally . . . will stand. . . . Will we be true to our last-days, foreordained mission?"[120]

Well, will we?

Will we stay seated in the less-than-royal, bumpy train when so many other princess sisters are being deceived? When they forget their birthrights

119 Bradbury, William B., "We Are All Enlisted," *Hymns*, no. 250.
120 In Ashton, Marvin J., "Stalwart and Brave We Stand," *Ensign*, Nov. 1989.

and seem to side with the dragon, it makes it just a little easier for him and a little harder for us.

When I was in high school, I worked with several misled princesses. We were all waitresses at a truck stop café. Working at this café was, by far, the best money I had ever made. The truckers were tired and groggy and loved to see a smiling waitress with a good attitude. I listened to their stories about the road and did my very best to be a great waitress. I liked my job.

But the other princess waitresses did not like their job. They seemed to not like very much at all. They especially seemed to not like me. Maybe it was that I never joined in their gossip. Or maybe it was that I didn't complain with them. Or maybe it was that all of *their* regular customers were now *my* regular customers.

Even though I knew the other waitresses didn't like me, I still tried to be their friend. My efforts were in vain, however, and I found out later that these waitresses had been talking meanly about me behind my back. They had even created what they considered to be a belittling nickname: *Princess Meg*.

Princess Meg, who is always smiling. Princess Meg, who is too good to gossip. Princess Meg, who stole all the regular customers.

And you know what? That didn't bother me.

Because I *am* Princess Meg. And I am on the happily-ever-after–bound train. It doesn't matter how often my princess status is questioned, because I know who I am. I don't need beauty magazines to increase that royal feeling. I don't need popularity or anyone to accept my princess standards. I don't need to live in luxury to know that I am a princess.

I am Princess Meg.

I am Princess Meg, and you are Princess You.

And we rarely have the right hair or the right clothes or the right make-up, but there's nothing we can do to change the fact that we truly are princesses. Our looks are not what make us true princesses. Not in the eternal scheme of things.

Dragon fighting, moat-less, tiara-less, we are still princesses—because we are daughters of Heavenly Father. President Dieter F. Uchtdorf reminded us: "You are truly royal spirit daughters of Almighty God. You are princesses, destined to become queens."[121]

And someday we won't cross paths with princesses on other trains or battle the dragons that threaten our seats. We will step off and receive a

121 Uchtdorf, Dieter F., "Your Happily Ever After," *Ensign*, May 2010, 127.

crown of eternal life,[122] our wage for our labor. It is a crown we'll never take off, a crown for the right princess who has done the right things.

Until then, we're here, "sandwiched," as President Uchtdorf said, in the pages of our story "between [our] 'once upon a time' and 'happily ever after.'"[123] We're still far away from our heavenly home, where our King awaits. We have promised to complete our mortal purposes and return to live with Him and to live like Him. We have every intention of keeping that promise.

And He knows it.

When I was a teenager, it used to bother me that Heavenly Father knew all things.[124] It bothered me that He knew the end of my story when I hadn't even written it yet.

One day as I was driving on the freeway, I thought about Heavenly Father and His all-knowingness, and I began to get frustrated, even a little angry. I wondered why Heavenly Father had sent me down here to prove myself when He already knew how my story would end. It bugged me that He already knew what choices I would make and how I would react to, well, everything.

My eyes narrowed as I drove. *Why is He wasting my time?* I thought. *Why doesn't He just tell me so I don't have to disappoint Him if I fail? Why is He putting me through this anxiety?*

But something in my soul stirred.

I gripped the steering wheel tightly with both hands. I decided that if I was the writer of my story, *I* would be the writer of my story.

Boldly, I prayed: *Heavenly Father, if You really know how this all works out, and if You really know the end of my story, then You know I'm gonna make it! If You really know all things, then* that *is what You know!*

At that moment, my heart exploded with a joy that filled not just me but my entire car. It was as if Heavenly Father Himself sat beside me. I felt a sweet assurance come over me as if to say, "Yes, that is what I know."

Our happily ever after can be a sure ending because *we* are the writers. We hold the pencil. As we zoom down the tracks, seat-belted on the train with dragons breathing hot, sticky breath onto the window beside us, we write the pages of our stories.

We rarely get to write the beginning lines of each chapter in our lives, which seem to always be foreboding literary phrases like, *It was a dark and*

---

122   See D&C 20:14.
123   Uchtdorf, Dieter F., "Your Happily Ever After," *Ensign*, May 2010, 125.
124   See 2 Nephi 9:20.

stormy night . . . or *She never suspected it, but . . .* but as the train rocks back and forth and the dragon claws our window, we grip our nubby pencil tighter and write more intensely.

That ending will come. Our train will reach its destination. And we will step off into our eternal homecoming, where we won't have to blow a kiss to our Heavenly Father anymore. We will hug Him. And we will write the last line of our story:

And she lived happily ever after.

About the Author

ARTIST AND AUTHOR MEG JOHNSON continues to motivate thousands of people across the globe with her motto "When life gets too hard to stand, just keep on rollin'!" Meg accidentally jumped off a cliff and broke her neck in 2004 and spent four months in the hospital recovering from multiple injuries. She returned home without the use of her legs, back, stomach, or hands—a quadriplegic. Meg knows that even though being physically paralyzed is hard, being spiritually paralyzed is harder. This book details the steps we can take to remain spiritually able.

Since being paralyzed, Meg has competed in the national Ms. Wheelchair America Pageant in New York, founded and directed Ms. Wheelchair Utah (and still directs it), and instituted a service outreach program for recovering hospital patients. Meg reaches people's hearts worldwide through her newsletter, "Meg's Monthly Message: A True Story from My Life to Help You in Yours." She received the Athena Award in 2012 for her service efforts. She enjoys her greatest accomplishment every day as she gets to be a wife to her husband, Whit.

To meet Meg, watch her videos, listen to free audio, or sign up for her newsletter, visit her on her website at www.MegJohnsonSpeaks.com.